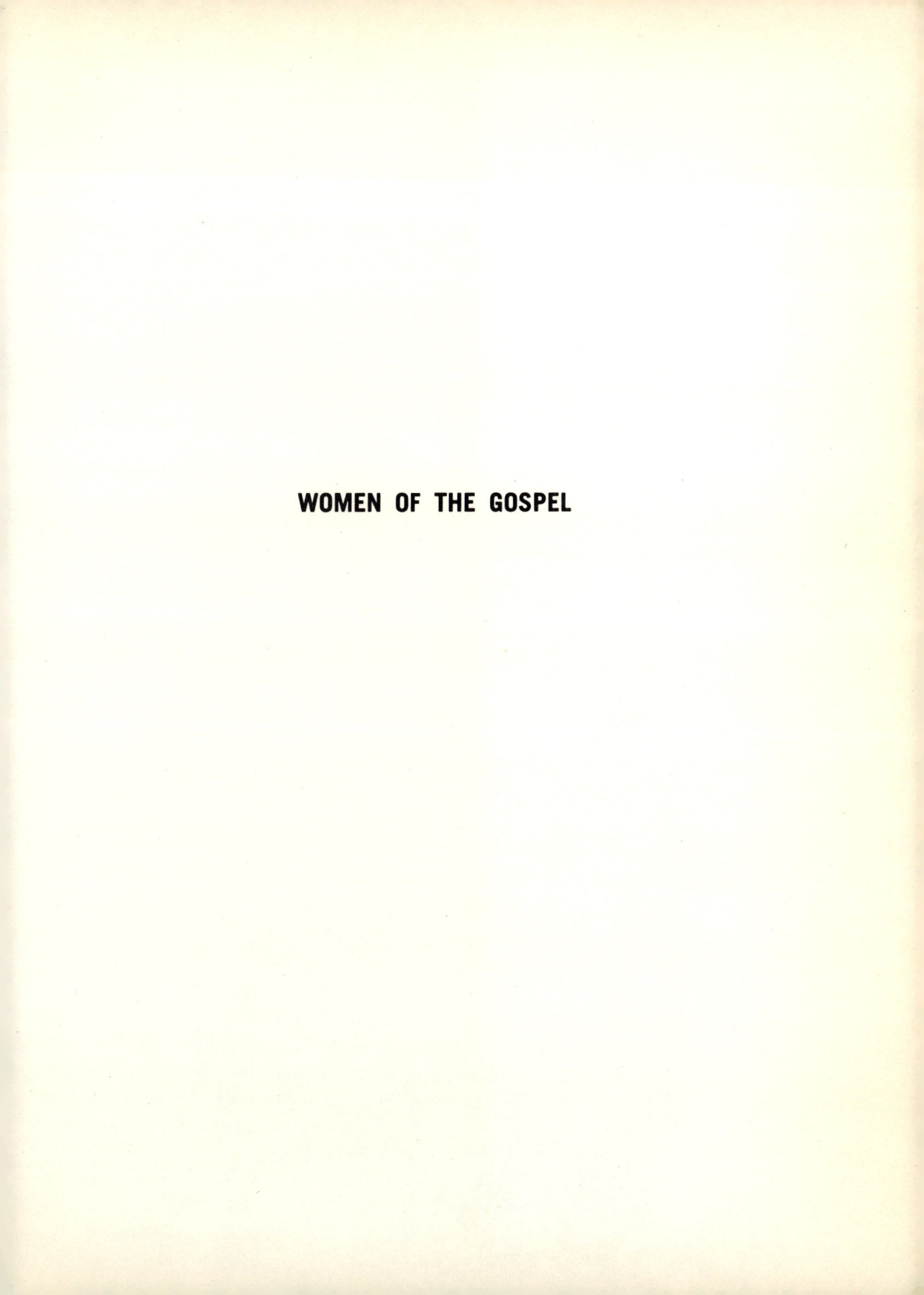

WOMEN OF THE GOSPEL

Simon Peter's
Mother-in-Law

Mary

The Woman
with a Hemorrhage

Mary of Bethany

The Widow of Naim

The
Syrophoenician
Woman

Claudia

The Samaritan
Woman

Mary Magdalene

The Widow
and Her Mite

Martha

An Unknown
Sinner

WOMEN OF THE GOSPEL

Written by the
Daughters of St. Paul

Illustrations by Gregori

ST. PAUL EDITIONS

Nihil Obstat:
  Rev. Msgr. John G. Hogan

Imprimatur:
  ✣ Humberto Cardinal Medeiros
  Archbishop of Boston

  January 15, 1975

Library of Congress Cataloging in Publication Data

Daughters of St. Paul.
  Women of the Gospel.

    CONTENTS: Elizabeth.—Mary.—Anna. [etc.]
    1. Women in the Bible. 2. Bible. N.T.—Biography.
I. Title.
BS2445.D38   220.9'2 [B]   74-32122

Scripture passages from The New American Bible, 1970, used herein by permission of the Confraternity of Christian Doctrine, copyright owner.

Copyright, © 1975, by the Daughters of St. Paul

Printed in U.S.A. by the Daughters of St. Paul
50 St. Paul's Ave., Boston, Ma. 02130

The Daughters of St. Paul are an international religious congregation serving the Church with the communications media.

CONTENTS

Elizabeth — She Beheld the Dawn	12
Mary — Handmaid of the Lord	18
Anna — Sincere Seeker	24
Herodias — She Used Her Power Wrongly	30
The Samaritan Woman — She Became a Missionary	36
Simon Peter's Mother-in-Law — Hers Was a Grateful Heart	42
The Widow of Naim — She Found Compassion	48
An Unknown Sinner — Love Gave Her a New Heart	54
Jairus' Daughter — She Met a Friend	60
The Woman with a Hemorrhage — It Took Courage	66
The Syrophoenician Woman — Firm Was Her Faith	72
A Crippled Woman — She Stood Up To Give Thanks	78
Salome — Love Would Find the Way	84
The Adulteress — Witness to God's Mercy	90
Martha — Loving Hands and Ready Faith	96
Mary of Bethany — Everything She Could	104
The Widow and Her Mite — The Greatest Gift	110
Claudia — The Message that "Failed"	116
The Women at the Cross — Faithful to the End	122
Mary Magdalene — After the Sunrise	128

elizabeth

SHE BEHELD THE DAWN

It was a beautiful day. As Elizabeth walked to her open doorway and paused to savor the contrast between the semi-darkness within and the splendor without, she was conscious of standing between the twilight of one era and the radiant dawn of another.

The new life stirring within her, a life foretold to her aging husband through an angel, was a pledge of a whole new age coming to birth. Perhaps as she gazed out at the rugged Judean hills that had beheld so many struggles of her people for land, liberty and fidelity to their God, Elizabeth recalled Isaiah's prophecy that the dry land would burst into bloom with the coming of the Messiah.

A marvelous promise made to her husband Zachary and communicated by him to her—

a promise rich in scriptural allusions—had heralded the new era. Elizabeth was to have a son in her old age, and that son was to turn the hearts of many Israelites back to their God. Even now, six months after the announcement, she could hardly believe it. But it was true....

She withdrew again into the cool of the house. Suddenly a pebble crunched; a slight figure appeared in the oblong doorway and stood silhouetted against the flaming hills.

"Peace be to you, Elizabeth!"

As if coming from the sun itself, young Mary of Nazareth stepped forward to embrace the aging matron. The infant in Elizabeth's womb leaped, and she was overwhelmed by a joyous realization that before her stood the Mother of the Messiah!

As a member of the priestly tribe, familiar with the Scriptures from childhood, Elizabeth responded to the divine impulse within her and uttered a greeting which has resounded down through the ages.

"Blessed are you among women!"

Unknowingly, she was repeating the praise given to Mary by the angel Gabriel only a few days before. In the name of all generations, Elizabeth added:

"And blessed is the fruit of your womb."

Then, as a sense of her own unworthiness gripped her, a torrent of exclamations poured from her lips—exclamations of wonder that the Lord's Mother had so eagerly come to see her, exclamations of praise for Mary's total belief in the divine promises made her through the mediation of an angel.

Radiant with the same joy that had given wings to her nimble feet, Mary replied with a canticle of thanksgiving. The "Magnificat" summed up all the love and longing of the "poor ones of Yahweh"—the *anawim*—for the God who had now descended into the midst of His people.

It was a scene never to be forgotten—this first homage paid by a human being to the Redeemer and His Mother, the Mother who always redirects the praises given her to the "mighty One who does great things."

After the birth of John, Elizabeth disappears from the Gospel, her mission of praise and prophecy ended. But those divinely inspired words of hers live on and on, and find an echo in the heart of anyone devoted to the Mother of Jesus:

"Who am I that the mother of my Lord should come to me?"

"Blest is she who trusted.... Blest are you among women.... Blest is the fruit of your womb" (Lk. 1:42-45).

ZACHARY'S CANTICLE

"Blessed be the Lord the God of Israel
   because he has visited and ransomed his people.
He has raised a horn of saving strength for us
   in the house of David his servant,
As he promised through the mouths of his holy ones,
   the prophets of ancient times:
Salvation from our enemies
   and from the hands of all our foes.
He has dealt mercifully with our fathers
   and remembered the holy covenant he made,
The oath he swore to Abraham our father he would grant us:
   that, rid of fear and delivered from the enemy,
We should serve him devoutly and through all our days
   be holy in his sight"
                              (Luke 1:68-75).

MARY

HANDMAID OF THE LORD

It was the turning point of history, the happiest day in the life story of mankind—and perhaps this is why the Author of the universe chose to shroud it in mystery. The angel Gabriel was sent from God to a small Galilean village, to a virgin betrothed to a man named Joseph. "And the virgin's name was Mary."

Who was Mary? A girl of perhaps fifteen, already greatly favored by the Most High. "She," writes Paul VI, "more than all the patriarchs and prophets, more than the just and pious Simeon, awaited and implored the consolation of Israel, the Christ of the Lord." We may well believe, then, that Mary was at prayer when God's messenger greeted her.

The angel's salutation was not the customary oriental greeting: "Peace." Rather, it was an exclamation that pealed out in praise of the divine generosity. Various are the translations of this joyous greeting:

"Hail, full of grace."

"Exult, exalted in grace."

"Rejoice, O highly favored."

"The Lord is with you; blessed are you among women," Gabriel continued.

What wonder must have filled Mary's heart as the angel continued to speak. Did she perhaps realize that what had made her especially pleasing in God's eyes was her wholehearted response to all the spiritual gifts He had lavished upon her? "It is well to bear in mind," writes the Holy Father, "that Mary's eminent sanctity was not only a singular gift of divine liberality. It was also the fruit of the continuous and generous cooperation of her free will with the inner motions of the Holy Spirit."

Gabriel's revelation of the incarnation of God's own Son was steeped in mystery—the mystery of three almighty Persons—a mystery completely unknown to the Hebrews. But Mary accepted his words, believing that, as the angel himself had said, "Nothing shall be impossible with God." She must have realized, however, that sacrifice and suffering lay ahead....

For an instant the whole of human destiny hung in the balance. But only for an instant. Then Mary said, "Behold the handmaid of the Lord; be it done to me according to your word."

"From that moment," writes Paul VI, "Mary consecrated herself entirely to the service not only of the heavenly Father and of the Word Incarnate, who had become her Son, but also to all mankind, having clearly understood that Jesus, in addition to saving His people from the slavery of sin, would become the King of a messianic kingdom, universal and eternal.... The whole life of the humble handmaid of the Lord, from the moment when she was greeted by the angel, until her assumption body and soul into heavenly glory, was a life of loving service."

Mary hastened first to visit and help St. Elizabeth. Then with Joseph she undertook the difficult journey to Bethlehem, where she brought the Infant Savior into the world. In Egypt and again at Nazareth, she devoted all her energies to common household tasks, meanwhile "pondering and keeping in her heart" all the marvels God had revealed.

During Jesus' public life, Mary remained in the background. Only on Mount Calvary—not on Mount Tabor—did she come forward to stand in silence and offer her Son, and herself along with Him.

Nor did Mary's mission end with the return of her Son to His Father. She who was the "summit of the Old Testament and dawn of the New" was to live in the heart of the infant Church, "shining forth to it as a model of all the virtues." Mary, who undoubtedly longed to leave this world and be with Christ, acted as mother and counselor of the apostles, as her Son had desired.

"Of all human beings," writes Pope Paul VI, "Mary offers the most shining example and the closest to us of that perfect obedience whereby we lovingly and readily conform with the will of the eternal Father. Christ Himself, as we well know, made this full closeness to the approval of the Father the supreme ideal of His human behavior, declaring: 'I do always the things that are pleasing to him.'"

In our materialistic age, which so needs faith and dedication, Mary's unwavering belief and lifelong obedience challenge us to shun mediocrity and reach for the stars.

"My being proclaims the greatness of the Lord, my spirit finds joy in God my Savior" (Lk. 1:46-47).

ANNA

SINCERE SEEKER

The great temple courts bustled and teemed with the usual noisy traffic. As a young couple made its way through that miniature city, the child nestling in His Mother's arms gazed upward with solemn blue eyes.

That small Galilean family appeared quite ordinary—although unusually devout, since Mary and Joseph had come in person for the rituals of purification and the redemption of the firstborn. Like the mother of Samuel, Mary intended to offer her child to the Lord.

Unexpectedly, an elderly man approached, his face alight with joy. The tradition of Mary's temple childhood suggests that she knew this aged Simeon.

Inspired by the Holy Spirit—who had promised he would live to see the Messiah,

25

ANNA — SINCERE SEEKER ANNA — SINCERE SEEKER ANNA — SI

the Consolation of Israel, the Salvation sent by God—Simeon held out his arms to receive the helpless Infant from His Mother. And with the Savior in his arms, he was prompted by the Holy Spirit to declare the Infant the Light of nations. Simeon's ecstatic words recalled several prophecies of Isaiah—salvation would be extended to the whole world!

As Mary and Joseph marveled at the old man's understanding of God's plan, Simeon, their elder, blessed them and spoke to Mary with fatherly concern. The Holy Spirit continued to enlighten him; he saw that the Light of the world would be God's suffering servant, a sign of contradiction and division. "A sword shall pierce your own soul," he said to her, implying that the divisions brought about by Mary's Son would result in misunderstandings, rejection and victimhood, in which she would share.

It was at that moment—as Mary began to live in a continual perspective of sacrifice—that another aged figure came forward.

Anna, a widow of the Galilean tribe of Aser, was well known to worshipers in the temple. She was one of those saintly souls who ever seek the peace of God in the midst of clamor and traffic. Honoring the liturgical observances, following the prescribed fasts, and performing the traditional practices of piety, she constantly implored the advent of the Messiah.

Anna's continual presence in the temple suggests that she had set up her own small cell in an inconspicuous corner, in order to live there night and day, a contemplative in the midst of feverish activity, "in the world but not of it."

As through Zachary and Simeon, so now through Anna, the age of preparation paid its tribute to the new era coming to be. Anna, too, was one of the *anawim*—God's poor ones—those of clean hands and pure heart who seek God totally, who cling to Him and to His will. And, in the tradition of Miriam and Deborah, she was a prophetess.

Upon seeing the Child Jesus, the elderly widow broke into exclamations of praise. The Holy Spirit told *her*, too, that this was the Savior!

Indeed, Anna's great joy led her to seek out all her friends who longed for the Messiah's coming. She told everyone about the Infant in the arms of Mary of Nazareth.

"Seek the Lord where he may be found"— so exhorted the prophets. This, Simeon and Anna did, in the spirit of the beatitudes.

Seeking Him sincerely, they found Him, just as today's seekers find Him in the Eucharist, in the Scriptures, in the sacraments and in the hearts of their fellow men.

"Happy are they whose way is blameless,
who walk in the law of the Lord...
who seek him with all their heart..." (Ps. 119:1-2).

herodias

SHE USED HER POWER WRONGLY

herodias was furious. She stalked up and down the royal chamber like a lioness deprived of its prey. That man, that John, had too much power over her husband! Right this minute, Herod was downstairs, listening to John speak about repentance. Had her own influence weakened so soon?

Herodias stopped pacing and stared out through a slit in the fortress' thick, stone walls. Stark sands and blistered rocks glared below, while to the west the Dead Sea steamed in the sun. Machaerus could be absolutely unbearable, she thought. How she wished to return to the royal court at Tiberias near the sparkling waters of Galilee! But Herodias knew that her husband was here in Machaerus for a reason—to defend his tetrarchy. Aretas, king of the Nabataeans, was certain to try to avenge his daughter, the wife Herod had repudiated when he returned from Rome with Herodias.

Herodias was not worried about Aretas, however. Rather, she feared and hated a **gaunt** figure clad in a camel skin who had

31

come from the fords of the Jordan to censure the tetrarch and his wife face to face.

Of course, Herod had been angered by John the Baptist's condemnation of their marriage. The tetrarch had even imprisoned the Baptizer. Yet Herod liked to listen to John....

How weak he is, thought Herodias. She would have to sway him, just as she had enticed him to take her from his half-brother Philip in Rome and bring her back to Palestine with him.

There had to be a way to remove the Baptist, she thought.

A burst of girlish laughter rang out in the corridor. Her daughter, of course, and some friends....

And Herodias knew what she would do.

The birthday of Herod the tetrarch was a great event. Invitations had gone out to Roman officers and leading citizens alike. Everyone in search of favors or a good time made his way to the grim fortress on those desolate hills east of the Dead Sea.

The banquet couches were filled; meal and entertainment began. At a special, well-timed moment a single dancing girl flashed in. She danced and danced, in the sensuous manner of the East, and the jewels on her lithe body danced with her. The guests applauded wildly and congratulated the ruler. Herod, overcome by wine, passion and flattery, cried out, "Ask for whatever you want, and I will give it to you."

The girl hesitated; the guests stared. Some, at least, were stunned by his rashness. But Herod would not back down now. He raised

3. Women of the Gospel

his arm, swore an oath and added, "I will give you anything you ask, even if it is half my kingdom."

Perhaps already suspecting what she should ask for, the girl hurried off to her mother. And Herodias did not hesitate. This was the moment she had waited for. "The head of John the Baptist," she hissed.

Herodias' daughter tripped back into the banquet hall, which became deathly silent. She stood before Herod, and suddenly her expression became stern, like her mother's. Eyes fixed on the tetrarch, she exclaimed, "I want you to give me—right away—the head of John the Baptist on a platter!"

A gasp went up from the men reclining on their banquet couches. As hard as most of them had become, they had never expected this. They gazed blankly at the tetrarch.

But Herod would not take back the oath he had made before so many witnesses. He could not endure such a humiliation. He called men and gave orders.

After a moment of incredulous buzzing, the hall became silent again. Herod's eyes were downcast. The guests' eyes moved from him to the girl standing motionless before him.

Minutes dragged by. Then heavy footsteps approached. A tall executioner entered the hall, carrying an object on a dish. He started to present it to the tetrarch, but Herod hastily motioned towards the girl, who stepped forward to receive it. Taking the dish in both hands, she hurried off to her mother.

Herodias had triumphed! Gone was the danger of Herod developing a conscience about their marriage. The royal power she

had schemed for, she now grasped firmly—
or so she thought.

Herodias contrasts strongly with such Gospel figures as the Samaritan and Syrophoenician women, Martha and Mary, the widow of Naim.... She stands out as an exception, reminding us that "a woman who hates ceases to be human" (Alban Goodier).

A woman's power over men and children can never be overestimated. Every woman in the world possesses tremendous potential for good or evil.

What became of Herodias? The Gospel tells us no more, but secular history picks up the narrative and relates that she became jealous of her brother, Agrippa, when the emperor gave him another portion of Palestine together with the title of king. She urged Herod to seek the same title for himself.

When the couple reached Rome to make their request, they discovered that Agrippa had sent agents on ahead to denounce them as rebels against the emperor. Herod was exiled into Gaul, where he and Herodias passed the remainder of their days.

"What did our pride avail us?
   What have wealth and its boastfulness
     afforded us?
All of them passed like a shadow
   and like a fleeting rumor;
Like a ship traversing the heaving water,
   of which, when it has passed, no
     trace can be found,
       no path of its keel in the waves"
   (Wis. 5:8-10).

THE SAMARITAN WOMAN

SHE BECAME A MISSIONARY

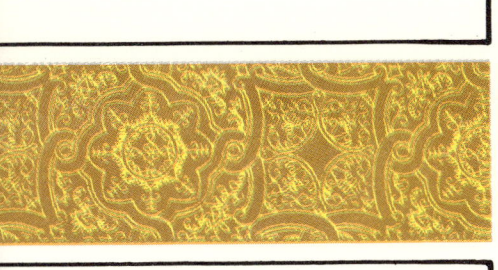

The afternoon sun beat down on Jesus and His apostles as they rounded a bend at the foot of a mountain and paused to gaze down a long valley. About half a mile ahead lay the town of Sichar, a series of square, white houses winding along the base of a ridge. Several hundred yards below the travelers lay a well encircled by low stones. This was Jacob's well, a landmark still famous among the Jews. Mount Gerizim, sacred mountain of the Samaritans, loomed across the valley.

They descended to the well, and the disciples left Jesus there while they went on to buy food in the village.

Jesus was tired. His public ministry had begun about a year before and had been filled with days of preaching and nights of prayer. The opposition to Him was soon to become more vehement, culminating in His passion and death.

This thought must have been continually with Him on His journey from the lower Jordan valley to the Galilean hills.

As Jesus rested, a woman from the village approached, a water pot on her head. The method of carrying the vessel was normal, but the hour was strange; most women—together with their children—approached the wells in chattering groups during the cooler hours of morning and evening. Such solitary behavior would have suggested to anyone that this person was something of an outcast.

She hooked her vessel onto the well rope, lowered it, and drew it up again, all the while ignoring the man seated beside the well. Such was to be expected, for in the East a woman does not look at a man, much less a Samaritan woman at a Jewish man. Great was her surprise, then, when this man asked her for a drink.

She gave Him one, hesitated and then voiced her surprise: "How is it that you, a Jew, ask a Samaritan and a woman for a drink?"

Jesus' answer puzzled her still further, but it led her to think a little more deeply than usual.

"If you only knew God's gift," said Jesus, "and who it is that asked you for a drink, perhaps you would have asked Him, and He would have given you living water."

The woman's next question showed only a faint glimmer of understanding. "Sir," she said, "you have nothing to draw water with and the well is deep. Where does your

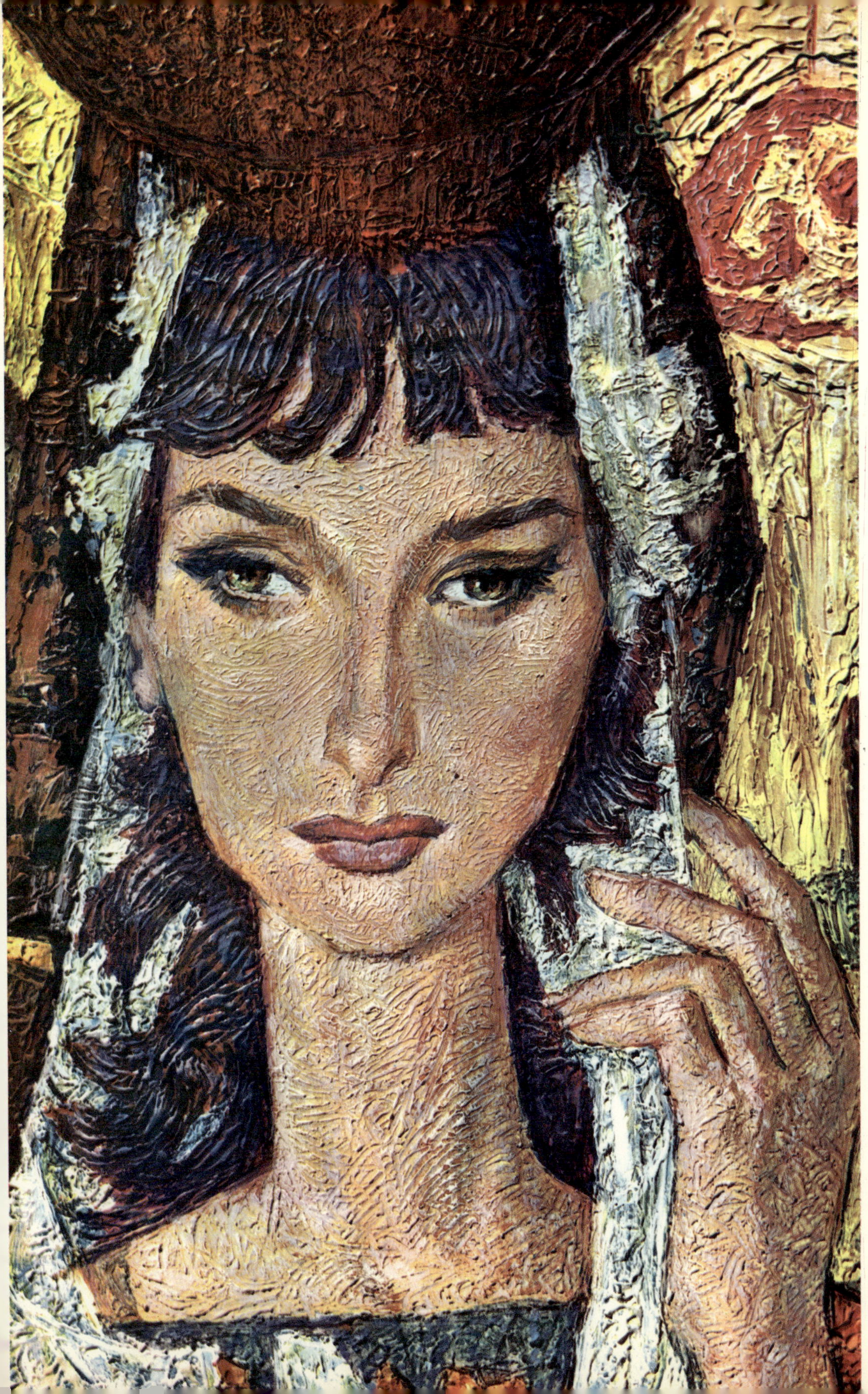

living water come from? Are you greater than our father Jacob who gave us this well?"

As Jesus spoke on—of living water rising up to give eternal life—she understood still less. Her own life was too far removed from things of the spirit. But this woman *wanted* to understand, and, like the dying thief who asked to be remembered in Jesus' kingdom, she made a simple act of faith: "Sir, give me this water, so that I may never be thirsty nor come here to draw it."

"Call your husband and come back here," Jesus replied.

She was caught off guard, but struggled to keep the stranger's esteem by telling Him a half-truth: "I have no husband."

"Well said," replied Jesus calmly. "For you have had five husbands and the one you have now is not yours. In this you were right."

With an embarrassed laugh and the affirmation that Jesus was a prophet, the woman admitted her guilt, only to change the subject at once and ask a question about divine worship.

Again, Jesus' reply was beyond her capacity, but she snatched at one thought: "The hour is at hand when true adorers shall adore the Father"—and replied: "I know that the Messiah is coming, who is called the Anointed One. When He comes He will teach us everything."

And thus this sinful Samaritan woman became the first person to hear from the lips of Jesus: "I who am speaking with you—am He!"

With the arrival of Jesus' shocked disciples, that poor woman hurried off to the village and became His first apostle. Heedless of what anyone would say or think, she called out to one person after another: "Come and see a man who has told me everything I have ever done. Isn't he the Christ?"

Brief though that meeting had been, her life would never be the same. By responding according to her capacity, she had become a missionary who would never forget that ringing declaration: "I who am speaking with you — am He!"

"With joy you will draw water
 at the fountain of salvation, and say on
  that day:
Give thanks to the Lord, acclaim his name;
 among the nations make known his deeds"
  (Isaiah 12:3-4).

SIMON PETER'S MOTHER-IN-LAW

HERS WAS A GRATEFUL HEART

Simon Peter, who had first met Jesus of Nazareth many months before on the banks of the Jordan River, was now one of His regular followers. At the Master's call, Peter and Andrew, James and John had left their boats and nets to move about with Jesus as He preached—now in a synagogue, now on the lakeshore of Genesareth, now on a hillside behind Capernaum.

There was a mysterious fascination about Jesus that made people suddenly forget their ordinary, daily routine to hear in the voice and read in the eyes of this tall, young preacher the echo and reflection of something wonderful almost within their reach....

James and John may not have been sure what their father, Zebedee, thought of their sudden response to Jesus' call, and probably

Peter, too, wondered how he should explain it to his mother-in-law. Perhaps it was to reward her consideration, as well as to show his gratitude for the Master's friendship, that Peter invited Jesus to dinner that Saturday.

Among the most vivid descriptions in the whole Gospel are the accounts given by Mark and Luke of that particular Saturday in Capernaum.

The day began in the synagogue with Jesus preaching and His countrymen marveling at His words and His authority. Then, as the crowd began to pour out of the lamp-lit hall, like a typical Sunday-morning church congregation, a shriek rent the air: "Let us alone! What do we have to do with you, Jesus of Nazareth? Have you come to destroy us?"

He who had raised this cry was a familiar sight in Capernaum. Yet never had the townspeople seen this lunatic act quite as he did now; never had they seen something like the fires of Gehenna smoldering in his eyes.

"I know who you are—" the voice continued at a strained pitch—"the Holy One of God!"

Jesus did not let the possessed man speak further. "Stop this!" He exclaimed. "And go out of him!"

The lunatic's body began to writhe. Then it cast itself to the floor in the center of the chamber and lay still.

Beneath the wondering gaze of all, the contorted face relaxed. Slowly the man sat up, then rose to his feet. He was without a scratch and completely sane.

"What *is* this?" murmured the throng. "What new teaching?"

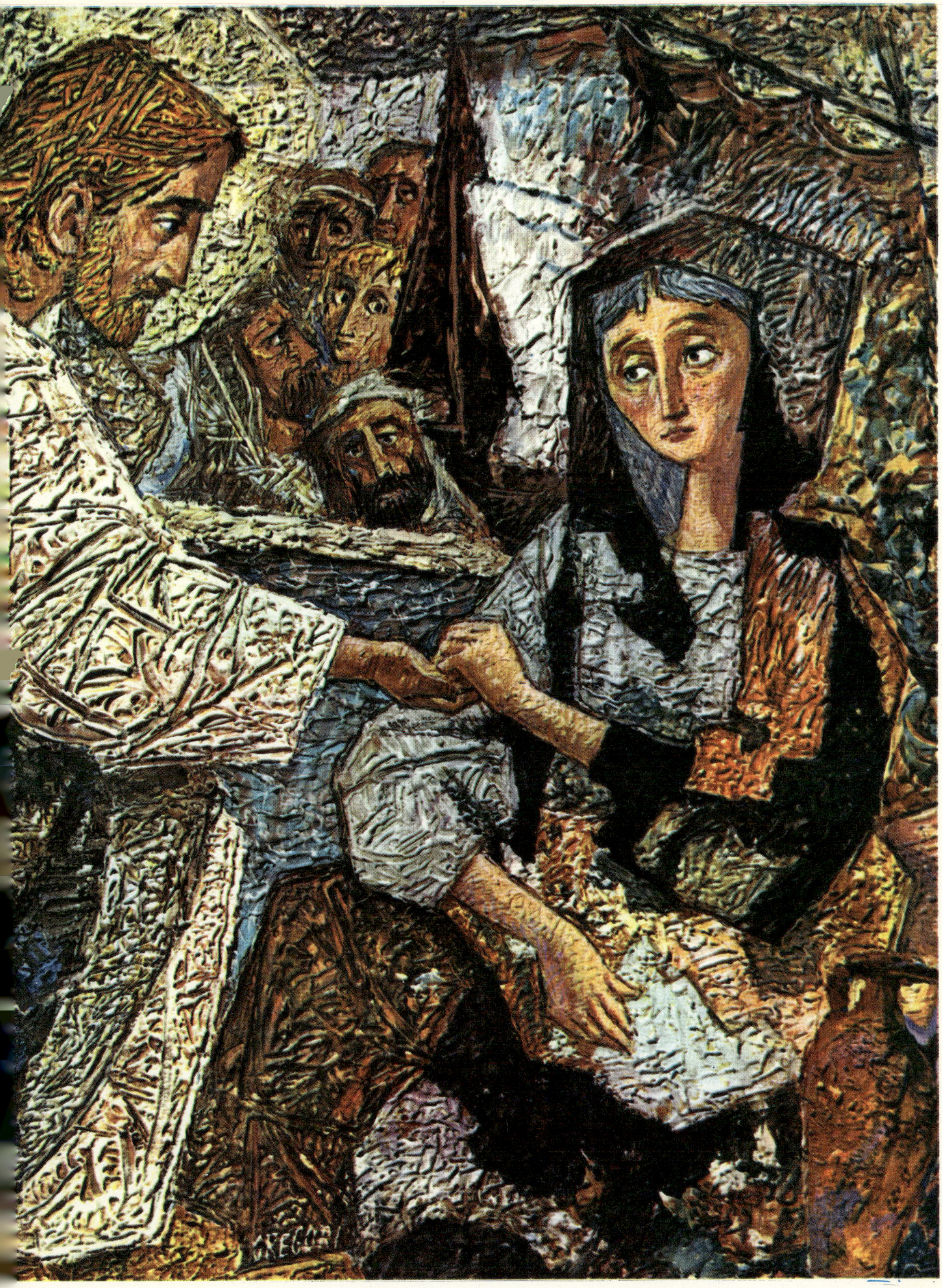
GREGORI

"With authority he commands even the evil spirits and they obey him!"

Still buzzing, the throng moved out into the street and broke into smaller groups, which wove their way homeward through lanes and by-ways. Jesus and His four walked toward Peter's cottage, not far from the lakeshore. The Master had His own lodging in Capernaum, but Peter had extended an invitation that He was pleased to accept.

At the cottage, however, they were greeted by the news that Peter's usually tireless mother-in-law had taken to bed with a raging fever.

The disciples looked at one another. Then they looked at Jesus. At Cana several months before, hadn't He changed water into wine? And but a few weeks ago, over a twenty-mile distance, hadn't He cured the dying son of a royal official? And this very morning, not even an hour ago, hadn't He driven the devil out of a man possessed?

"Rabbi," they said, humbly yet confidently, "her fever is dangerously high."

Jesus entered the sick room and drew near that poor form, bent and shivering beneath a mound of coverings, its face red, its eyes glassy. He took the woman by the hand and pulled her up. And as Jesus did so, Peter's mother-in-law felt the shivering and throbbing stop and the dizziness subside. The fever had left her, as it had been commanded to do.

Jesus and His silent, awe-struck disciples returned to the outer room.

Only a few moments later, their hostess appeared and began to serve the meal. She was as bright-eyed and energetic as she had ever been. How eager she was to serve Him who had granted her this favor! This episode, many authors say, shows that God's favors should awaken a generous response.

News of the day's second wonder sped from house to house. Who did not have someone diseased, someone crippled or mentally deranged? Might not this young prophet—who had shown Himself so willing to heal others—might He not likewise heal their own?

It was still Saturday—the Sabbath. There were restrictions on the carrying of burdens. But in the quiet of their homes people made plans and readied patients. And as the last red-gold shafts of sunlight probed Capernaum's lanes and alleys, every street in the city began to stir.

They wheeled them, carried them, led them, dragged them (in the case of those possessed), and laid them in lines on both sides of the lane leading to Peter's door.

When Jesus came out, His heart—which was, after all, a very human heart—must have leaped with joy. What trust they had placed in Him! Passing from one poor sufferer to another, laying His hands upon each of them, the Master cured them all.

In the lamp-lit twilight, Simon Peter, his family and his friends watched in stunned wonder. Surely it had been a day they would never forget. And surely no one was more grateful than she who had been His hostess; she had received far more than she had given.

"Bless the Lord, O my soul,
   and forget not all his benefits" (Ps. 103:2).

THE WIDOW OF NAIM

SHE FOUND COMPASSION

Jesus had again come to the border between Galilee and Samaria. As the sun began to dip over Mount Carmel and shadows rippled across the valley of Esdraelon, the Master and His disciples made their way toward the walled city of Naim, which stood atop a low ridge.

It was a happy procession, consisting of Jesus and twelve special disciples whom He had named on the Mount of the Beatitudes, together with other Galileans and men from Judea and Perea, Tyre and Sidon who had recently thronged a natural mountainside amphitheater to drink in those wonderful promises, "Blessed are the poor in spirit... blessed are the meek, the single-hearted, the peace-makers...."

4. Women of the Gospel

As the party drew near the arched gate of Naim, another procession filed out to meet them. The happy chattering of travelers enthusiastic about blind who now saw, lame who now walked, poor who now heard the Good News, faded away in an instant. A wail arose from the cortege that came forward from the shadow of the city wall.

Four of the men in the lead bore a white-sheeted corpse on a light bier made from two poles and a piece of matting. They were followed by a throng of women, wailing in that way peculiar to the East. Alongside trooped teenagers, and directly behind the stretcher swayed a mournful figure draped in widow's garb.

The two groups met, and Jesus gazed down into the stricken eyes, the anguished soul of that mother. He knew.... Not only was she a widow; this dead youth had been her only son.

"And the Lord," St. Luke tells us, calling Jesus by this title for the first time in his Gospel, "was moved with pity."

Jesus did not wait for anyone to ask a miracle. "Don't cry," He said to the woman. Numb with grief, not daring to hope, she stood still and waited.

As the Master reached out and touched the stretcher, its bearers halted. The crowd's wailing ceased. Everyone watched intently. May we not guess that one of the most concerned watchers was the Mother of Jesus herself? For surely St. Luke's detailed account came to him from an eyewitness who also understood the sorrow of separation.

All eyes were fixed on the Master as He said, "Young man, I tell you to get up."

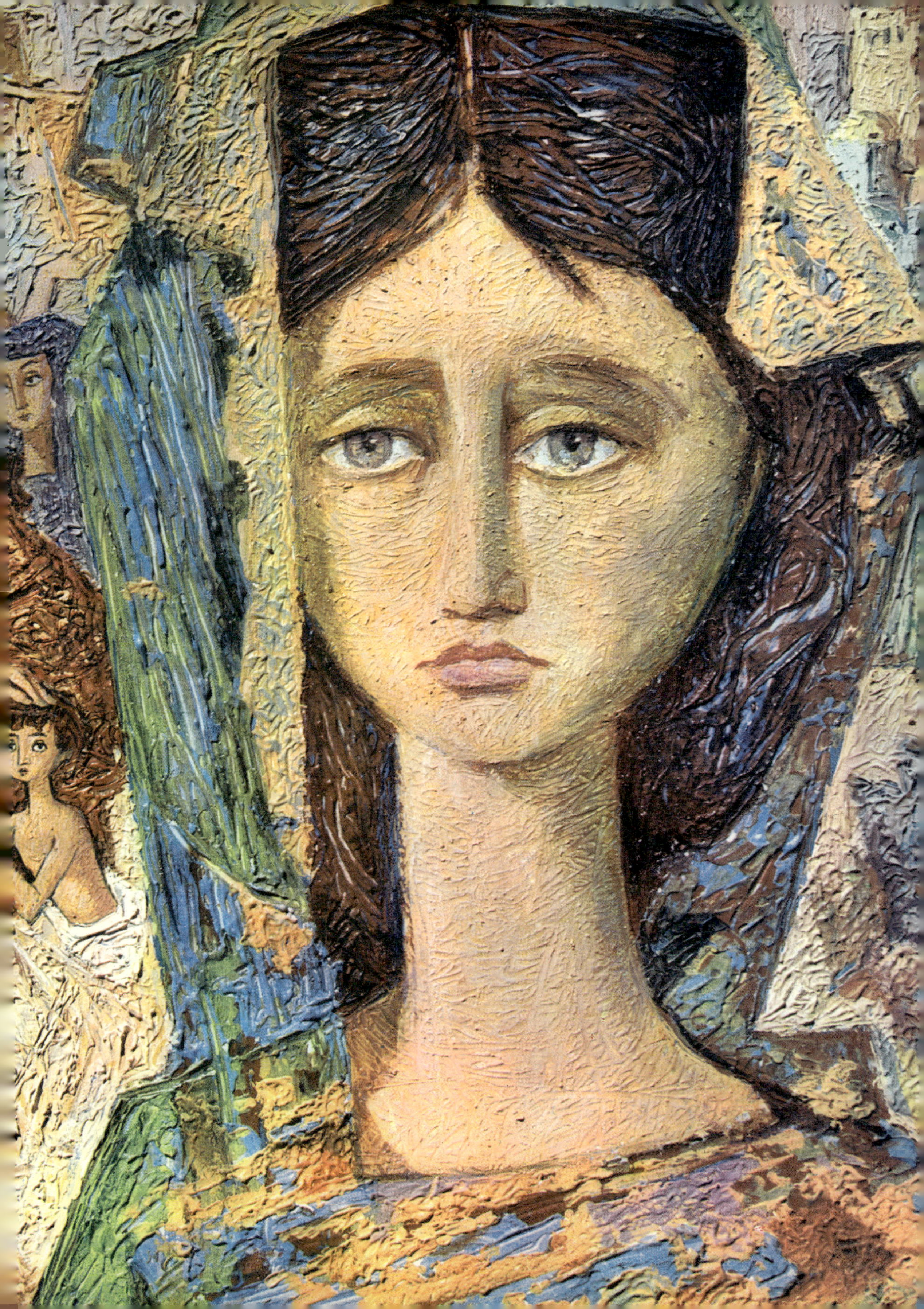

A tremor ran through the form on the bier; the corpse began to stir. It sat up and removed the cloth from its face. Bewilderment in his eyes and flush rising on his cheeks, the boy began to ask one question after another.

"Where am I? What's happening…?"

Slowly the astonished bearers lowered their burden to the ground, and the youth scrambled to his feet. Jesus led him to his mother, placing the boy's now-warm hand in her chill one.

As He did so, was He looking beyond, to Gethsemane, Golgotha and the garden of the resurrection?

The crowd swarmed about them, and everyone began to babble. Jesus' followers were telling the townsfolk about the miraculous cure of a centurion's servant and a mountainside sermon in which the Master had again spoken "as one having authority."

As He usually did when excitement was mounting, Jesus called His disciples and moved on. Voices behind them began to cry, "A great prophet has come among us!" For who had ever raised the dead before, save only the great prophets—Elijah, Elisha…? Yet not even they had raised the dead by a mere command…. "God has visited His people!" Could this be the Messiah? In joy not unmixed with fear, the word passed over the ridge, raced through Samaria and poured into Judea beyond.

"The Messiah! Has he come?"

Tongues wagged and friends rejoiced, while enemies became more bitter.

But to the widow of Naim only one thing mattered. The man named Jesus had understood her broken heart and healed it. Never would that mother forget the compassion in the eyes of the tall, young Rabbi who had said to her, "Don't cry."

He had again shown with His life what He repeatedly exhorted: to have compassion on the sick, the suffering, the oppressed, and give them a helping hand.

"Avoid not those who weep,
  but mourn with those who mourn....
Be generous to all the living" (Sir. 7:34, 33).

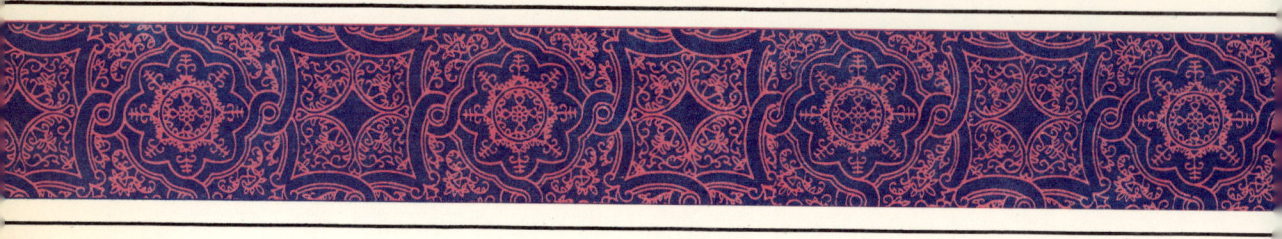

AN UNKNOWN SINNER

LOVE GAVE HER A NEW HEART

It had been a rather dull evening, thought Simon. He had been so eager to see and hear this young prophet from up in the hills. And he had been so certain that his dinner guests —the aristocracy of the town—would have been well entertained by Jesus of Nazareth. But not so.

I was right not to welcome him with ceremony, Simon reflected. There doesn't seem to be anything extraordinary about him at all. This uneducated carpenter, who carries on a very ordinary conversation, would not have known what to make of elaborate greetings. In the midst of us, he's out of his element....

A stir swept around the table, and out of the corner of his eye Simon glimpsed a swift movement. Still reclining in the oriental fashion, he raised himself on his elbow and craned his neck to see who had come to stand—or rather, to kneel—at Jesus' feet. He blinked, then gasped.

A woman of evil repute had stolen in from the terrace. Now she was crouching at the feet of the prophet from Nazareth. In one hand she held an alabaster box, which could only contain expensive, perfumed oil. What was she doing here—and with that ointment?

In an instant the alabaster box lay on the floor; the kneeling woman, overcome with emotion, was drenching Jesus' feet with her tears. Then, looking embarrassed, as if she had not meant to break down this way, she fumbled to unbind her long, flowing hair in order to dry the prophet's feet. Once more, emotion overpowered her, and as she wiped His feet she kissed them again and again. Finally she broke open the box and gently anointed them.

Jesus, Simon and all the guests had watched in silence. But the woman did not run off in shame. She remained at the Master's feet, waiting….

Who was she? To Simon, she was a known sinner. To Jesus, she was a penitent who had wholeheartedly accepted an inspiration to seek forgiveness. To us she is a model of what conversion really means—a change of heart.

The Gospel does not establish her identity. Early Christian writers believed she was Mary Magdalene, one of the women who later accompanied the Master and His disciples on their travels. Others hold that this woman, once converted, returned from Galilee to a small village outside Jerusalem

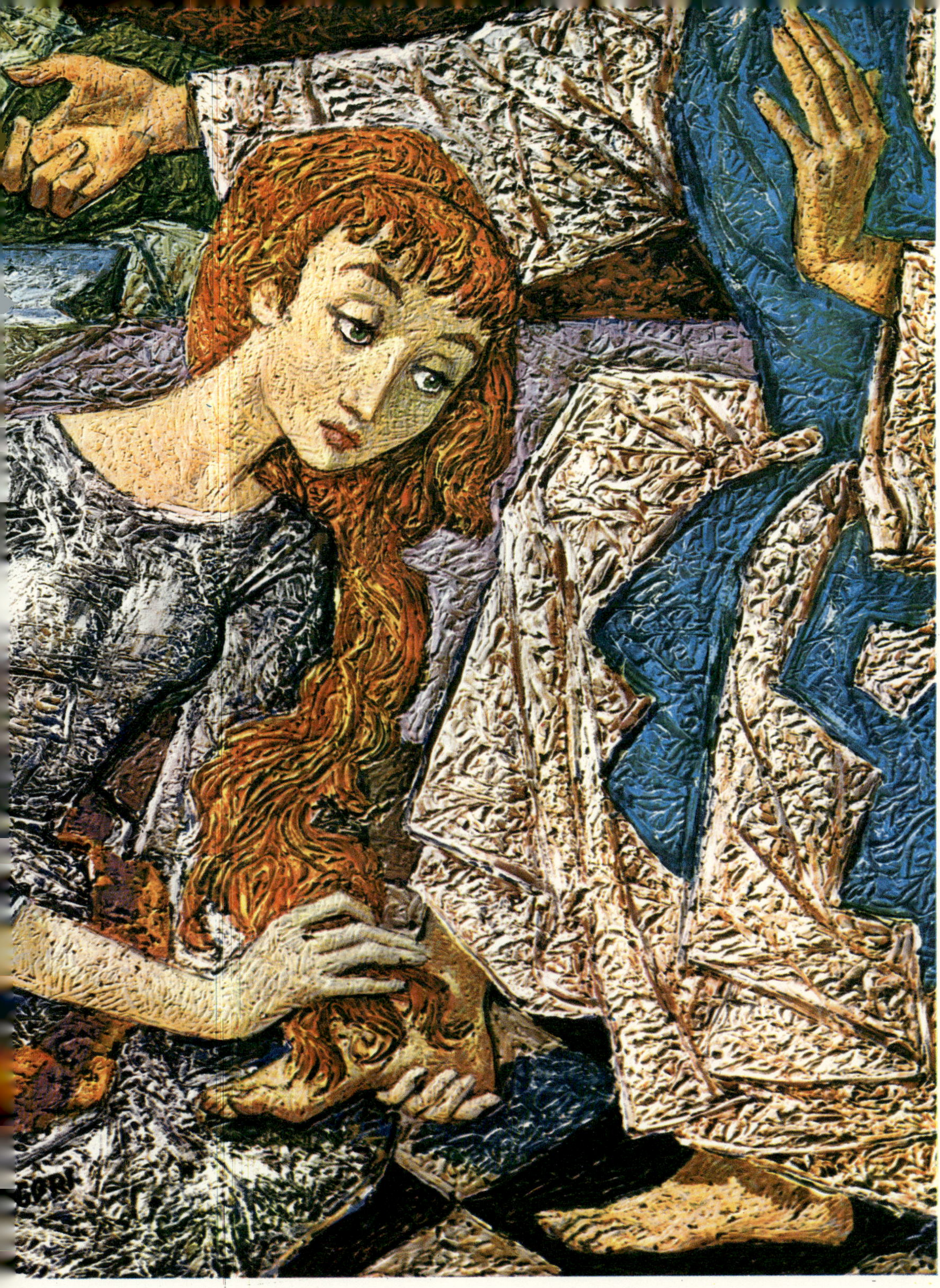

where she was reconciled to her sorrowing brother and sister. In other words, they believe that this penitent sinner was Mary of Bethany. But whoever she was, her impulsive deed will never be forgotten.

After the first stunned silence, the guests began to buzz.

Simon remained quiet, but in his heart he pondered. How could this man be a prophet if he let such a creature touch him? Surely a prophet would realize who and what she was!

"Simon," said Jesus, "I have something to say to you."

"Say it, Master," Simon replied. Now, perhaps, the mystery would be solved!

But Jesus did not mention the woman. "Two men owed money to the same moneylender," He said. "One of them owed five hundred coins; the other, fifty. Since neither could pay, he released both of them from the debt. Which of them, do you think, was more grateful?"

"I suppose the one who was released from the greater debt," Simon replied a little uneasily.

"You are right," the Master answered. Then He nodded towards the woman. "Do you see this woman?" And point by point He showed how generous she had been with Him. Simon had not offered Jesus the customary water for washing His feet. She, instead, had offered the water of her repentant tears and had gone so far as to use her own hair to dry His feet. Simon had not given the customary kiss of greeting. She, rather, had kissed Jesus' feet again and again as a sign of love and humility. Simon had not anointed his guest's head with ordinary oil. She, on the other hand, had anointed His feet with a costly ointment. Not one of this woman's gestures of affection and homage had gone unnoticed by the Master.

Then Jesus continued, "So I say to you that her many sins are forgiven because of her great love."

For the first time, He now turned and spoke to her directly. "Your sins are forgiven," He said. "Your faith has saved you. Go in peace."

He did not have to tell her to sin no more. He had read her heart.

"A clean heart create for me, O God,
   and a steadfast spirit renew within me."
(Ps. 51:12)

Jairus' Daughter

SHE MET A FRIEND

He loved his daughter so much; she was the apple of his eye. Jairus, ruler of the synagogue of Capernaum, would have done *anything* to keep his child from dying. And so, he threw himself at the feet of the famous young rabbi who had just returned from the far side of the Sea of Galilee. He prostrated himself before Jesus of Nazareth.

"My little daughter is very ill!" exclaimed Jairus. "Please come and lay your hands on her so she will get well." At once Jesus, accompanied by His disciples and a great throng, set out with Jairus through the narrow streets. A great crowd slowed their progress, and the incident of the woman who "touched only the hem of his cloak" halted them altogether.

It was just at this point that members of Jairus' household elbowed their way through the throng to tell him the dreaded news: "Your daughter has died. Why bother the Master further?" There was something of a sting in their words—a suggestion that the

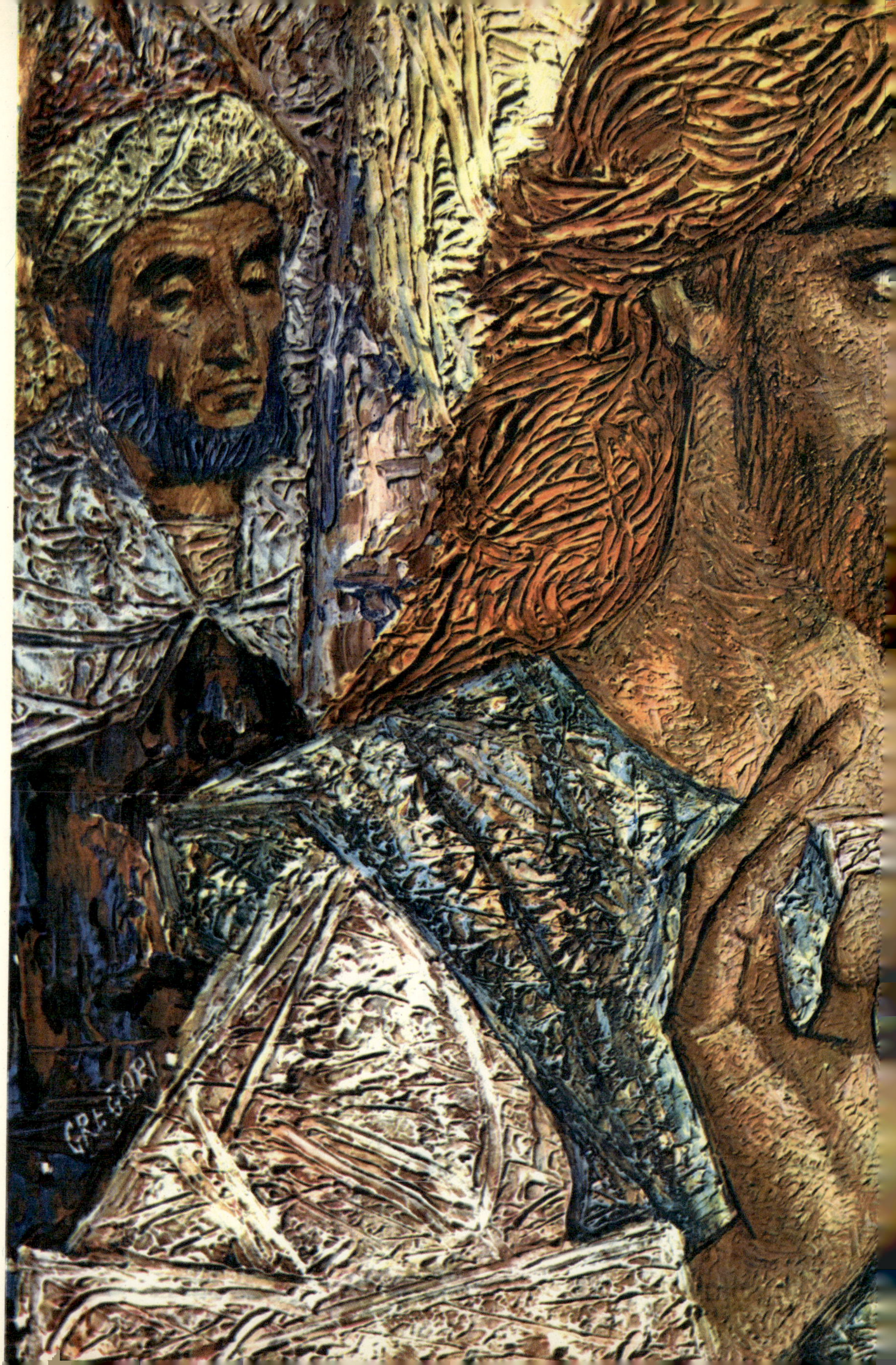
GREGORI

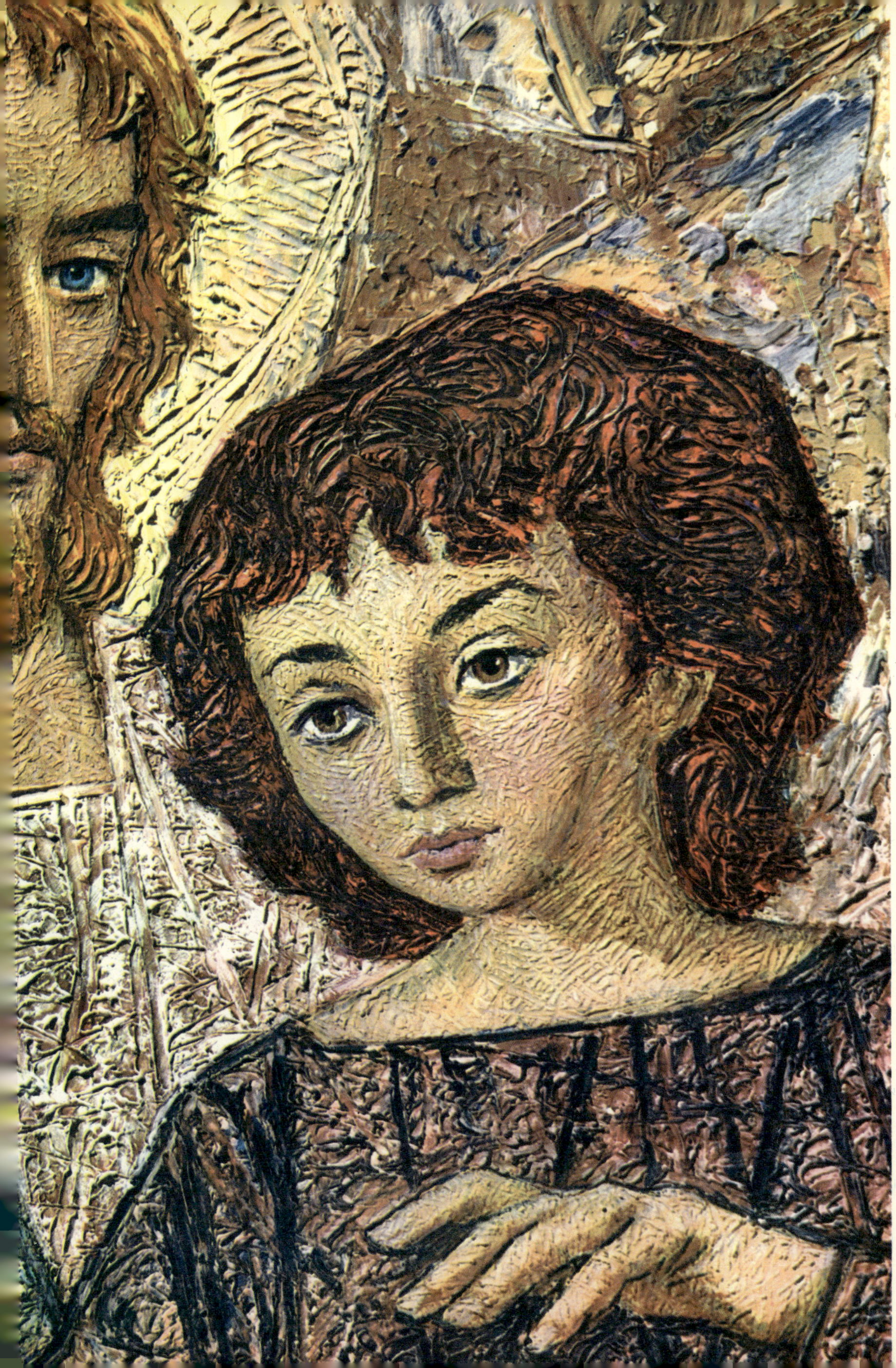

Master could have prevented her death had He really tried.

Jesus looked at Jairus. The official stared at the ground. That child had meant everything to him....

"It is useless to fear," Jesus said gently. "What is needed is trust."

Jairus' eyes flew open and gazed up into His. The Master *did* care, then. He *would* help—even now!

They pressed on through the city to the gate of the official's suburban home. There Jesus dismissed the crowd. No one was to enter the compound with them and join in the mourning, even though this was customary. His disciples, too, were to remain outside, except for a chosen trio: Simon Peter, James and John.

As He entered the wide courtyard, what a sight met the Master's gaze! All about sat women with disheveled hair and cold eyes—the hired, professional mourners of the East. They shrieked, they wailed, they uttered cries of agony, they groaned. And all the while the flute players added to the din.

The Master halted and looked about.

The mourners grew quiet. They knew who He was.

"Leave, all of you!" Jesus said. "The child is not dead. She is sleeping."

A wave of scornful laughter was their reply. The mourners could only be skeptical of the Master's mission and His miracles. Yet they dared not defy the fire in those eyes of His! Muttering and grumbling, the mourners withdrew.

Jesus found Himself with Jairus and his wife, some servants and close relatives, and the three apostles. Tearfully, the girl's parents led the Master and His chosen three into the little room off the courtyard where the child had been laid out.

She was as pale as wax, all wrapped in white with flowers strewn about her. The Master reached down and grasped one of those small hands, exclaiming as He did so, "Get up, child!"

The youngster's body quivered; her face flushed. She opened her eyes, and—with the Master's help—stood up at once and walked to her astonished parents.

Jairus stared at her, stunned. He had trusted, yes, but never had he dreamed that the child would be restored to him in an instant! Wasn't this very different from the way Elijah and Elisha had prayed for other dead youngsters to be brought back to life?

The girl smiled at Jesus, as children generally did. She could tell He was her Friend. "Give her something to eat," the Master directed. Having returned to life, the child would need nourishment, and in their excitement her parents were likely to forget that!

Then Jesus and His apostles left, directing the synagogue ruler to say nothing. Being God, the Master had ways unlike the ways of men. Genuine sorrow and simple trust always found a ready echo in His very human heart, but hypocrisy and empty show He saw for what they were. Perhaps this is why young people of every era have found Him to be their Friend and their Brother.

"Blest are the single-hearted,
   for they shall see God" (Mt. 5:8).

5. *Women of the Gospel*

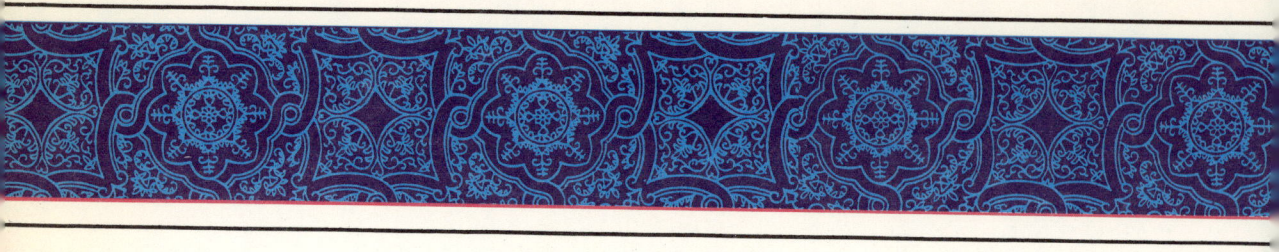

THE WOMAN WITH A HEMORRHAGE

IT TOOK COURAGE

The noisy crowd pressed up the narrow street, carelessly jostling one another and jostling Him who strode forward in their midst. The Master was hastening toward the home of Jairus, a ruler of the synagogue, for Jairus' daughter was at the point of death.

As the leaders of the throng rounded a corner, they brushed by a pale, worn woman standing close to the alley wall. She was waiting for the Master—waiting to touch the tassel of His cloak and be cured of an illness that had afflicted her for twelve years. Made legally unclean by her infirmity, she knew herself unworthy to approach the young rabbi. Hence the decision to touch just the tassel of His cloak; this would be enough.

Around the bend the clamor swelled, and she knew He would come by any instant. Yes

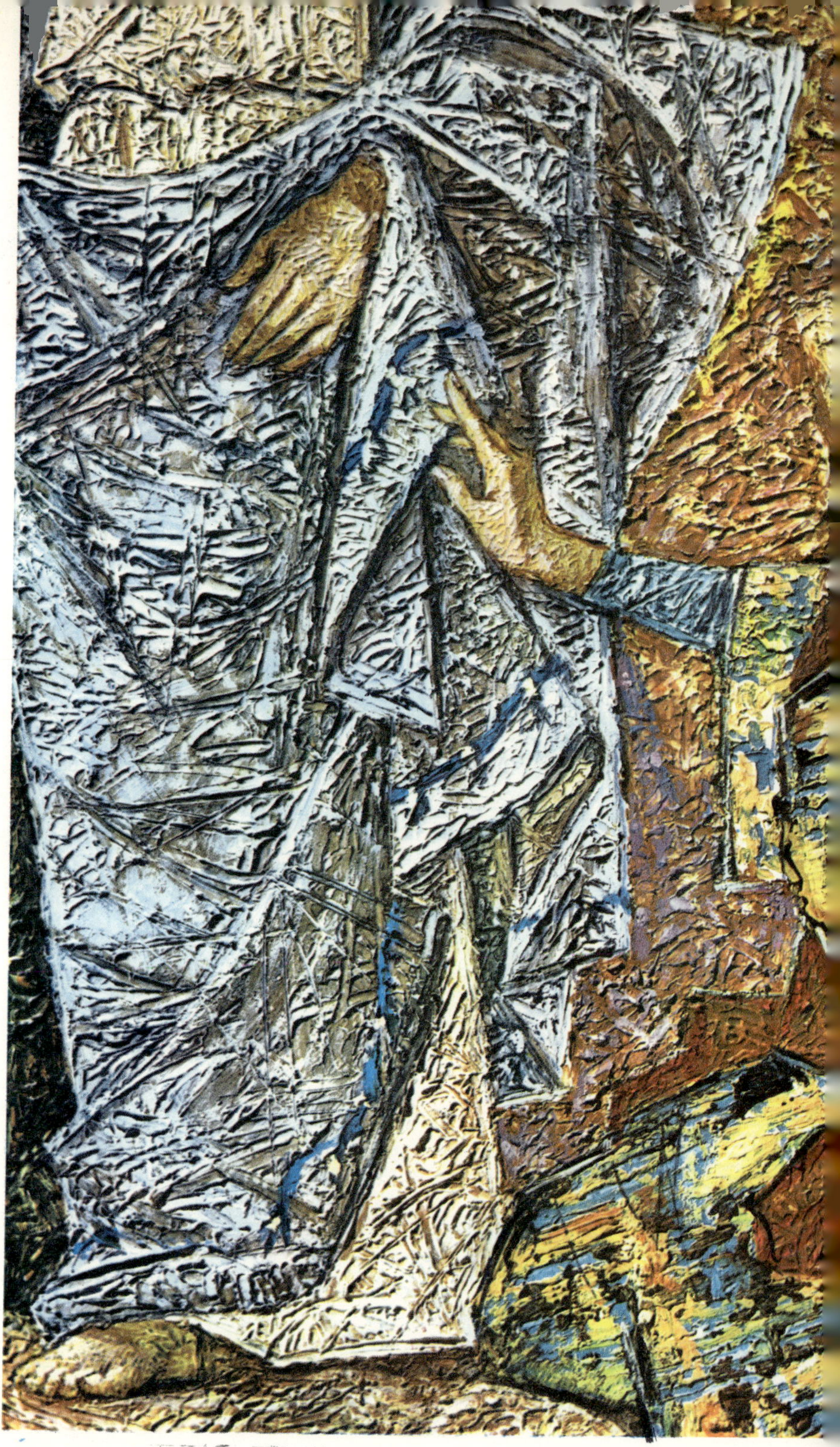

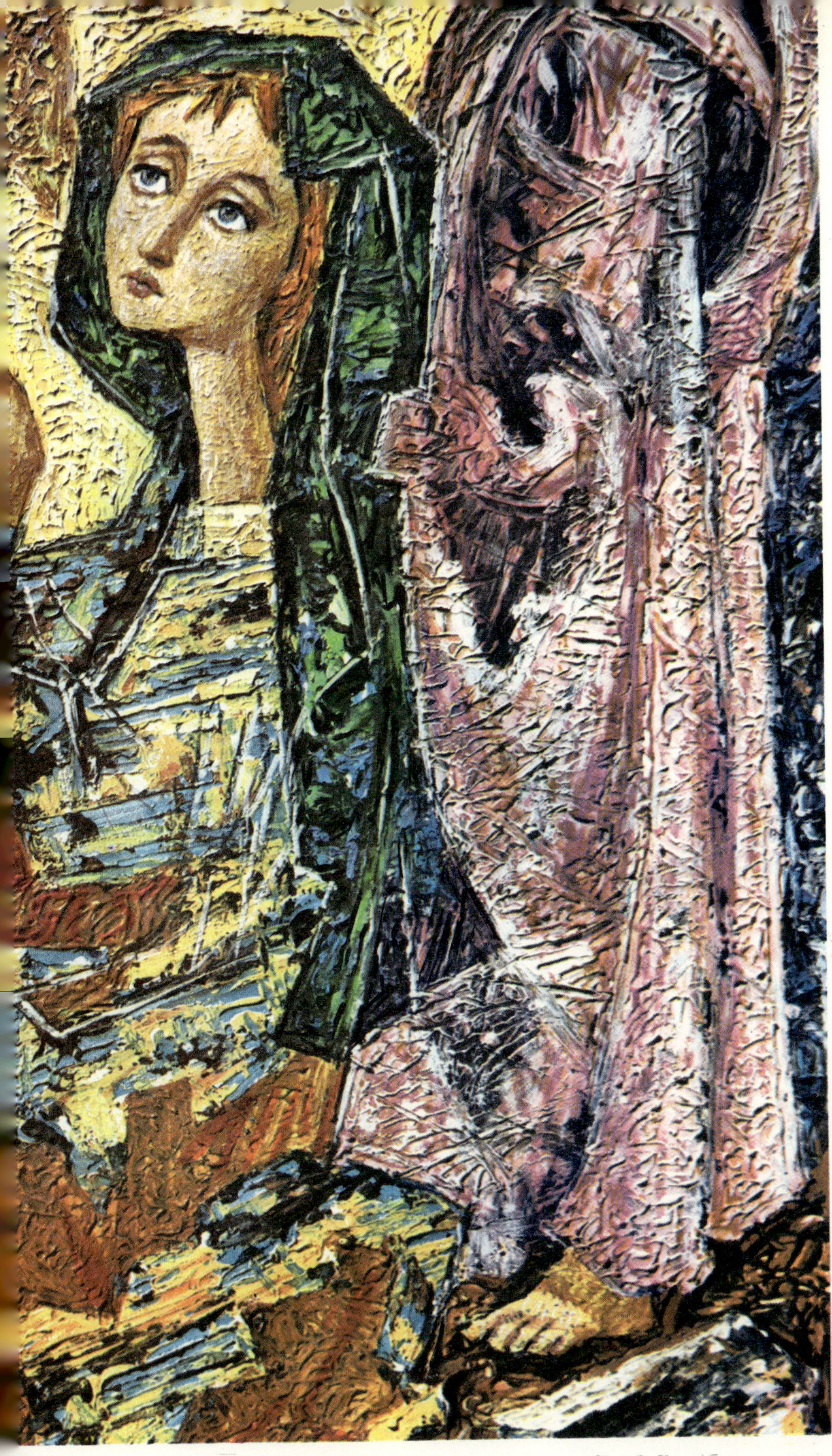

—there He was! In an alley where scarcely five people could have walked abreast, it was easy for her to reach out a trembling hand, clasp the tassel, withdraw her hand again and shrink back against the wall, waiting for the crowd to pass on.

But what had happened? First, the wonder she had desired. She felt herself healed! But secondly, the Master had stopped. As the crowd behind Him pressed forward, Jesus looked about, searching the faces of those close by. He seemed unusually serious, and the apostles wondered what had happened.

After a moment, the Master asked, "Who touched my cloak?"

What a strange question that was! Hadn't men been knocking and jostling Jesus all the way up the street? As He journeyed through towns and villages, wasn't Jesus always being bumped and even almost crushed by eager, impetuous throngs? And now He had asked who touched His cloak. Peter couldn't understand it—and he said so:

"Master, you see the crowds pressing in on you, and do you ask, 'Who touched me?'"

But Jesus said again, "Someone has touched me, for I know that power has gone out from me."

The woman, meanwhile, remained silent. Perhaps she hoped that someone else would step forward and acknowledge touching Him in order to be healed. But no one else did. Rather, those closest to Jesus had moved back a little, as if to assure Him that no one would touch Him again.

She was terribly afraid. Did Jesus regard the power that had gone forth from Him as stolen? Was He angry? Would He allow her infirmity to return to her?

She also felt ashamed. She did not want to speak of her illness in the midst of a mixed crowd.

Yet there was nothing else to do. Jesus had a right to know whom He had healed. And if He already did know, He had a right to be told of her gratitude.

By now, the throng had packed itself tightly about that tiny open space before Jesus. But the woman managed to push her way forward until she fell, trembling, at His feet. In a few seconds she had poured out the whole story, and how relieved she felt to see the smile of gratitude in His eyes. Yes, the Master was grateful, for He knew what courage it had taken for her to tell all.

"Daughter," He declared, "your faith has made you whole. Go your way in peace and be healed of your illness."

The early Christians saw in this woman a model of humility as well as of faith. She might also be considered an example of courage, for it takes courage to tell the truth when we fear what others will think or say. It was Jesus Himself who elicited this act of daring from her; once again, someone who approached Him in faith returned from the encounter a better person.

"The Lord is my light and my salvation;
   whom should I fear?
The Lord is my life's refuge;
   of whom should I be afraid?" (Ps. 27:1)

THE SYROPHOENICIAN WOMAN

FIRM WAS HER FAITH

The tide had turned in the life of the Master. He had emerged from obscurity to become the hero of Galilee, but now the relentless opposition of pharisees and herodians was taking its toll. The people were confused. Jesus went into the pagan district of Tyre and Sidon, where He would have more time to instruct His twelve closest followers in the kingdom of God.

In that district lived a poor woman whose daughter was possessed. She was Syrophoenician, as pagan as any Greek of her time. But some of her Jewish acquaintances, not long returned from Capernaum and the Mount of the Beatitudes, had told her about Jesus, the "Son of David," who could do wonderful things.

And she had believed them. How happy she was to learn that He was now in their district!

There was no time to lose. She knew where He was staying. Having asked a neighbor to watch over the sick girl, she made ready to find the man from Nazareth.

But she did not have to seek. He was passing by, right in front of her little hut, moving down the street in leisurely fashion with His disciples, making the most of this precious opportunity to continue their instruction. And immediately she began to cry out, "Have pity on me, Lord, Son of David!"

Strange words, these, from a pagan. But she had learned them from her Jewish neighbors and thought they would best express her confidence in His power.

Jesus, however, made no reply.

"My daughter is possessed by a demon," she continued.

Still Jesus was silent. He continued on with His disciples.

Another person might have been daunted. But not this woman. After all, the Master had not sent her away! With renewed courage, she followed along, crying out, "Lord, Son of David, have pity on me!" until the apostles could no longer concentrate on what the Master was saying.

"Send her away," they suggested. "She keeps crying after us."

"I was sent only to the lost sheep of the house of Israel," Jesus remarked. But He did not send her away. Rather, He kept walking and talking until He reached His lodging and entered it. And she followed. The next thing the disciples knew, she had

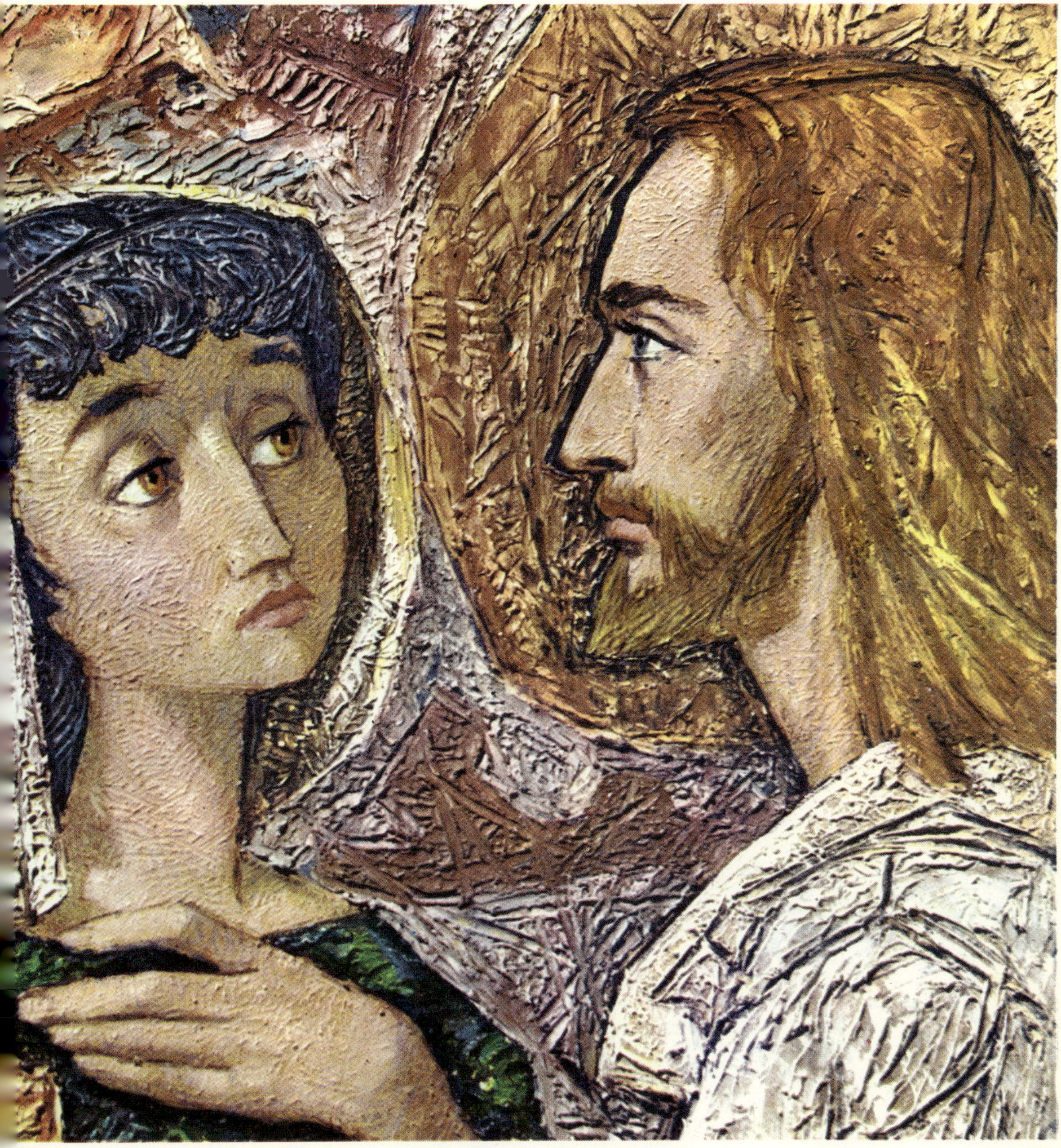

thrown herself on the floor at the Master's feet, as they sat in a circle around Him.

And with utter trust she looked up into His eyes and begged, "Lord, help me."

Calmly but gently, He told her, "It is not fitting to take the children's bread and throw it to the dogs."

The kindness of His tone dispelled any sting the remark could have contained. And it gave her still more courage. She had a ready wit, and now it served her well.

"Yes, Lord," she replied, recalling that dogs do belong to the household in their own way. "This is true. But the dogs that are under the table eat the crumbs that the children drop."

All she was asking was a "crumb." He who had done so many wonderful things would surely do this little favor!

"Woman," said Jesus, "you have great faith. For such a reply, be on your way. The demon has already left your daughter."

"Oh, thank You, Lord, thank You!"

She knew it was true. He had done it, as she had known He would. Radiant, she scrambled to her feet and hurried back to that poor, single-room hut where the girl lay on the bed, sound and well.

Spiritual writers say that the conditions for prayers to be answered are humility, confidence and perseverance. For two thousand years the Syrophoenician woman has given Christ's followers an example of all three. Jesus Himself told us to: "Pray without ceasing.... Ask.... Seek.... Knock..." not in the manner of the proud pharisee who does not know he needs God, but like the humble publican who knows how desperately he needs Him.

"Blessed be the Lord,
    for he has heard the sound of my pleading;
    the Lord is my strength and my shield.
In him my heart trusts, and I will find help;
    then my heart exults, and with my song I give him thanks" (Ps. 28:6-7).

A CRIPPLED WOMAN

SHE STOOD UP TO GIVE THANKS

Winter rains had begun to fall in Palestine, and barren hills were drinking in new life. The peoples of the Jordan valley, too, drank in new life, as Jesus of Nazareth journeyed through Perea and eastern Judea, preaching in one synagogue after another.

Jesus' newest followers multiplied quietly and steadily. They lacked the wild enthusiasm of those Galileans who had quickly forgotten about His feeding the five thousand and had returned to their fields and shops to walk with Him no more.

The Master worked fewer miracles among these southern shepherds and townsfolk, for pharisaical influence in the region was great. On the other hand, His sworn enemies were more cautious in their opposition, for they sensed that His following was loyal.

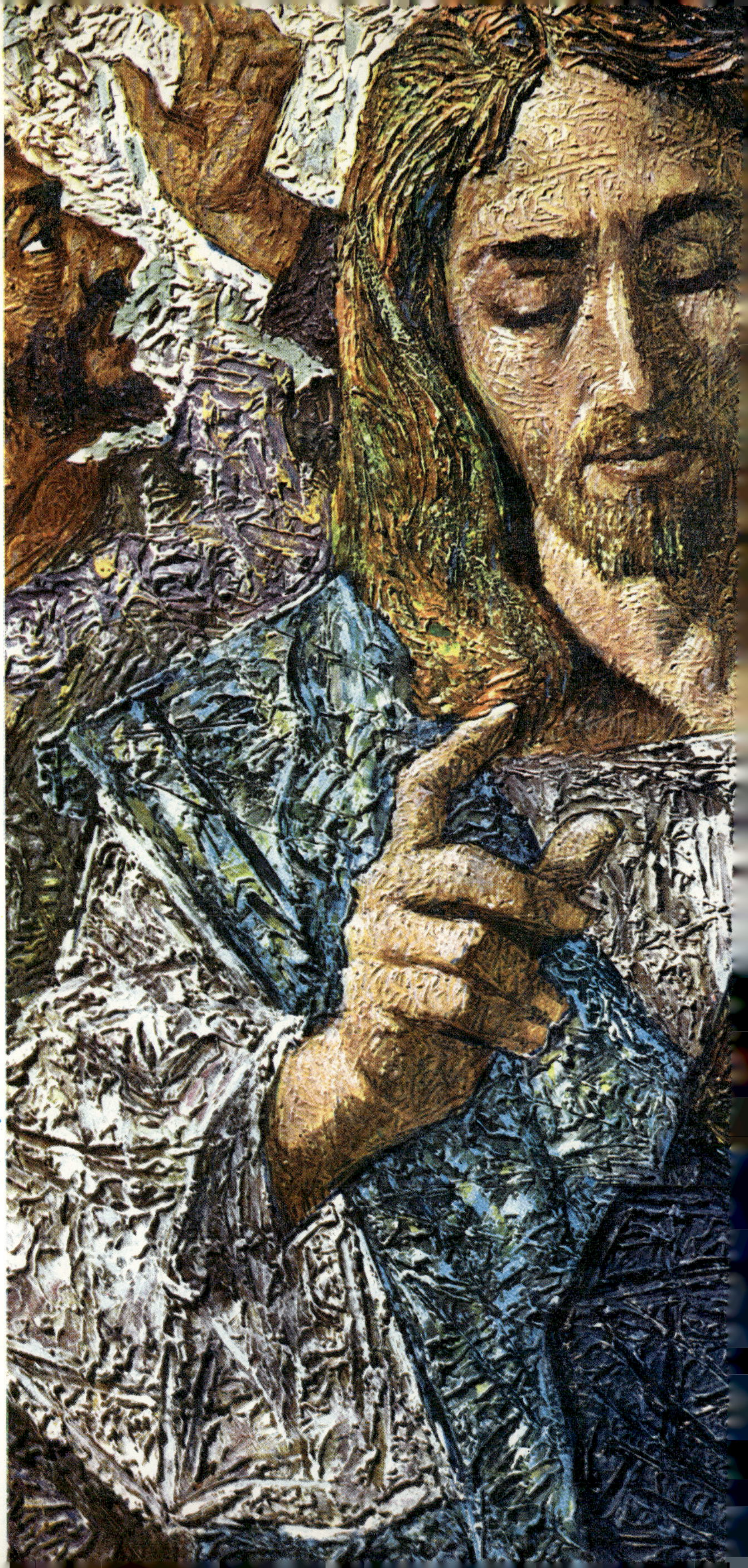

Women of the Gospel

Jesus devoted the greater part of His time to prayer and the teaching of His disciples. On Saturdays He entered the synagogues to preach.

During His discourse on a particular sabbath, a bent figure caught His eye. The woman was a pitiful sight, leaning upon a stick, unable to lift her head. She had held the same bowed position for eighteen years.

The townspeople thought that her illness had resulted from sin. It was the outlook of that era; the handicapped and retarded were to be shunned rather than regarded as objects of God's special love. Christianity was to bring a change in that outlook.

Jesus was aware of this prejudice. He also knew that today was the sabbath, on which no form of work was lawful. And yet, He called her.

She leaned heavily on her stick as she hobbled over to Him, head and eyes down.

Without waiting to be asked, without eliciting any act of faith, the Master said, "Woman, you are set free from your infirmity." He laid His hand on her shoulder, and at once she straightened up. Eyes shining with joy, she began to praise God.

The ruler of the synagogue looked on, perplexed. Whatever would his colleagues say? This young rabbi had healed on the sabbath (something that ordinary bonesetters were forbidden to do!) and in the synagogue itself. The ruler felt he must protest, and yet the prestige of Jesus—whom he had allowed to preach—prevented him from reproaching the Master directly.

So, turning to the people, the chief of the synagogue exclaimed, "There are six work days in the week. Come to be cured on one of them—not on the sabbath!"

The woman fell silent, but her face was still radiant.

Jesus turned toward the ruler and his cohorts. "O you hypocrites!" He exclaimed. "Is there any one of you who does not let his ox or donkey out of the stall on the sabbath to water it?"

No one answered, and the Master continued, pointing to the now-straight figure of the woman. "Should not this daughter of Abraham have been freed from her shackles on the sabbath?"

As the opposition grew silent, everyone else in the hall began to praise the Lord, who hides so many things from the proud and shows such goodness to the lowly.

"Then will the eyes of the blind be opened,
   the ears of the deaf be cleared;
Then will the lame leap like a stag,
   then the tongue of the dumb will sing"
   (Is. 35:5-6).

SALOME

LOVE WOULD FIND THE WAY

How happy I am, Salome mused. Lately, the Master has been taking the Twelve aside more and more. They must be making plans for the founding of His kingdom!

The clear gaze of Zebedee's wife rested on the majestic figure of Jesus, seated on a rock near the roadside, ringed about by the special group of disciples whom He called "apostles." The other disciples and the Master's faithful women followers were resting nearby. This had been a welcome stop on their journey down the Jordan valley to Jericho.

A stir swept through the little group of apostles. What had the Master told them? Salome wondered. But she knew she would not have long to wait; James and John, her sturdy sons, would tell her all.

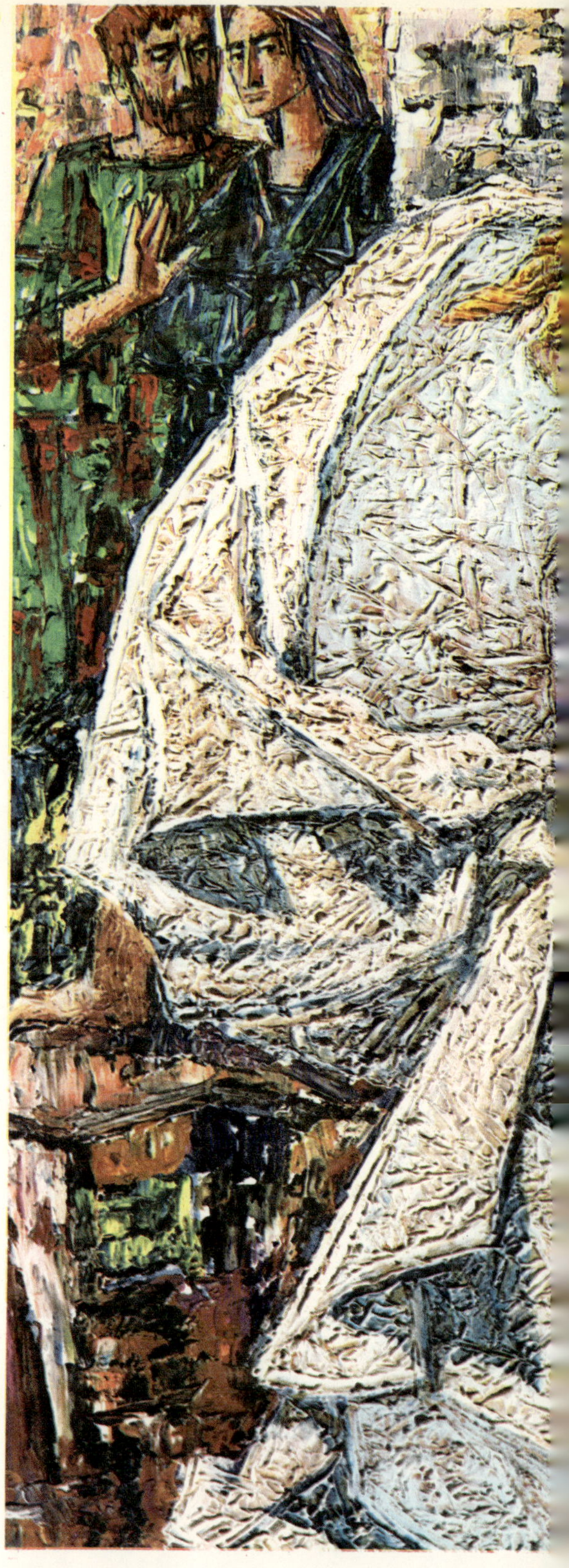

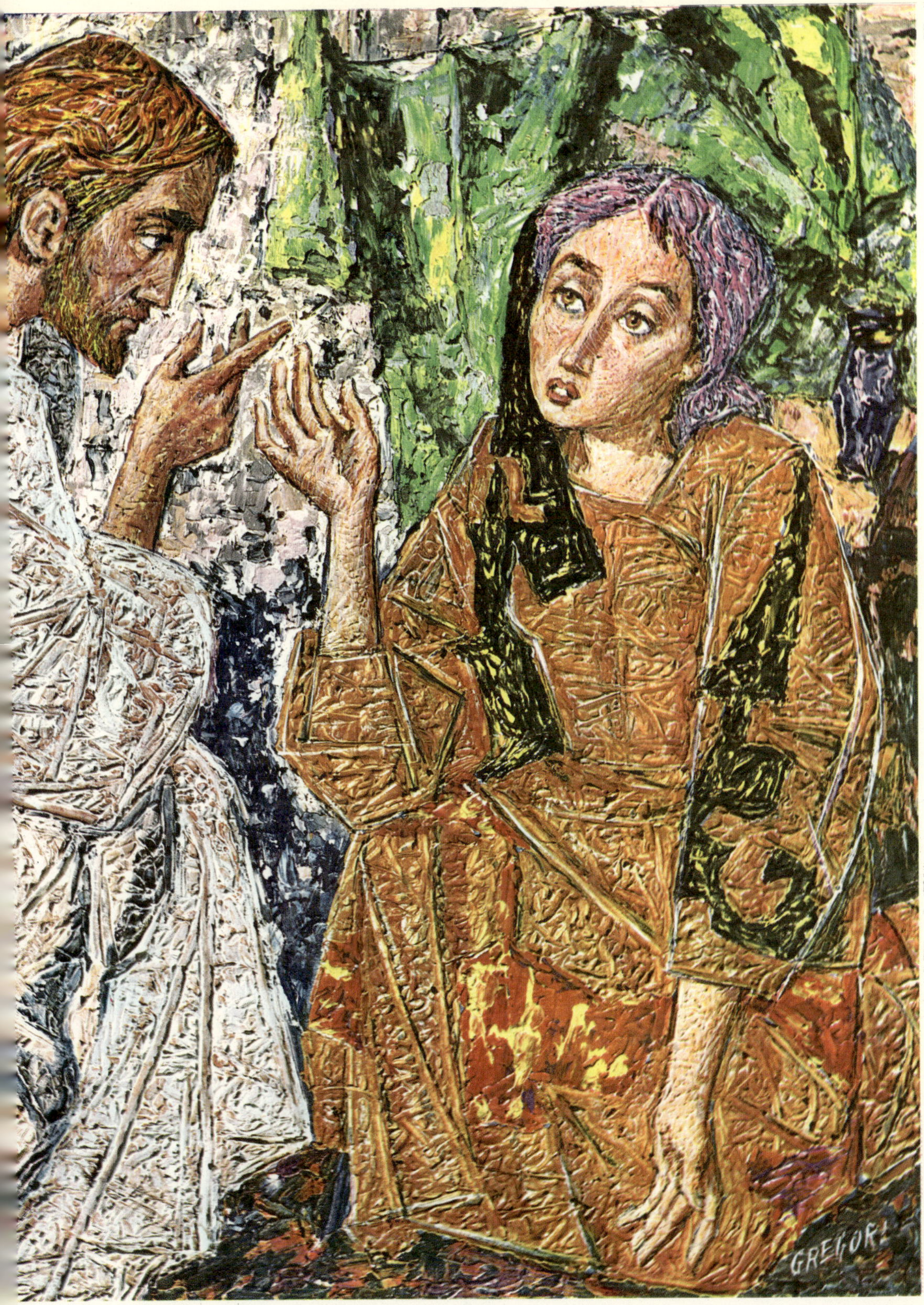
GREGORI

"He spoke again about suffering and rising," replied John to the silent question in his mother's eyes. "It was just what He said before. But now it seems nearer...." Both young men looked puzzled.

"Perhaps He's about to found His kingdom," Salome suggested. "And you will be at His right hand and at His left."

Bright smiles flashed across sun-bronzed faces. Indeed, shouldn't it be so? Even though Jesus had nicknamed the impulsive duo "Sons of Thunder," even though He had reproved them for wanting to call down fire from heaven to destroy a village of inhospitable Samaritans, even though He had chided John for not wanting to let outsiders expel demons in the Master's name—still the great wonderworker had shown special affection for Salome's fiery sons. Hadn't He allowed only them and Peter to witness the restoration of life to Jairus' daughter? And hadn't He chosen only these same three apostles to behold some secret revelation on a mountain top in Galilee—a revelation that James and John had not felt at liberty to describe even to their mother? Naturally, they should be first in the kingdom that was to be established!

At the moment, Jesus was alone. Should they not ask Him now, and assure themselves once and for all of their privileged position? With one accord and with ill-concealed excitement, the wife of Zebedee and her sons hastened over to the Master.

"What do you wish?" Jesus asked kindly. And all three blurted out their request—that James and John might sit at the Master's right and left hand in His kingdom.

The young prophet's reply was gentle, for He knew how attached to Him these three were. "You don't realize what you are asking," He chided gently. "Can you drink from the cup I am to drink?"

The Sons of Thunder hesitated only for an instant. They were aware that Isaiah, Lamentations, Ezekiel and the Psalms referred to the cup as an image of suffering. But they loved the Master and wanted to follow Him anywhere.

"We can!" they declared. And Jesus agreed that truly they would drink the cup. But, He added, what they were asking had to be granted by His Father, not by Himself.

Angry murmurs indicated that not all of the remaining apostles had been beyond earshot. "Come here, all of you," called the Master. And just as He had already told the Twelve that they must be like children in order to enter the kingdom of heaven, so now He declared that whoever wished to be the greatest among them must serve all the rest.

Mother and sons grew silent. They had so much yet to learn, but love would find the way. Both Salome and John would stand near the cross at Calvary, and, perhaps as a reward, they were to behold the marvel of the empty tomb. And James would be the first of the Twelve to die for Jesus.

Salome's dream of her sons' association with the Master in glory was to come true in a manner she had hardly suspected.

"We do not fix our gaze on what is seen but on what is unseen. What is seen is transitory; what is unseen lasts forever" (2 Cor. 4:18).

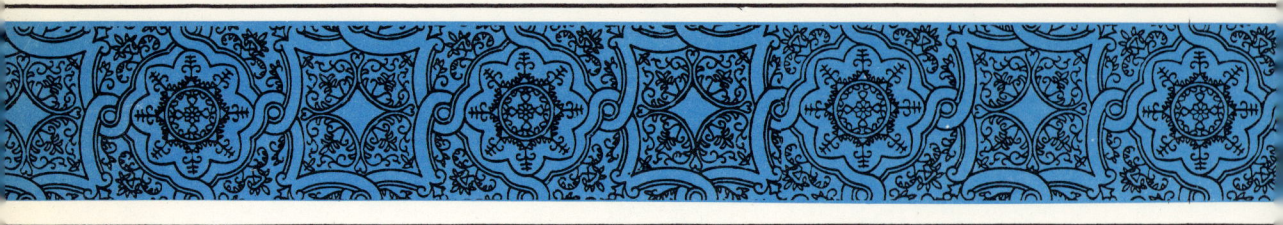

The Adulteress

WITNESS TO GOD'S MERCY

A pre-dawn twilight penetrated the Kidron Valley, softening the blackness of the olive groves. "Peter! James! The Master is ready!" Shadows stirred into life beneath the trees on the slope facing Jerusalem. Jesus' disciples rose to their feet, brushed themselves off, and began to follow their Leader down the narrow road. As the silent band crossed over the brook Kidron and climbed toward the city, Herod's magnificent temple loomed above them, sharply outlined against the paling sky. Behind it could be glimpsed the tower of the Fortress Antonia, symbol of Roman domination.

It was a disquieting scene, for several unpleasant clashes between the Master and the pharisees had taken place within those walls, beneath that tower. And more were likely to come today....

Already the temple area was astir, for at this time of year the Holy City swarmed with pilgrims. Jesus' reappearance was hailed with enthusiasm; never had anyone spoken as this man! As the people began to surround Him, He sat down and resumed teaching.

Suddenly the Master's calm, strong voice was drowned out by an excited babble.

"Make way! Make way!" The crowd parted hastily.

"Over here, you!"

"Stand right there in front of Him!"

Jesus gazed up into the crafty, mocking eyes of those who had made themselves His enemies. The pharisees had returned. In their midst trembled a woman they had herded before them with cries and insults.

"Master," hissed one, "this woman" (he pointed from a distance so as not to become legally unclean) "has just been caught in the act of adultery. Moses said to stone such women. What do *You* say?"

This was interesting. Seldom did these pharisees call Jesus "Master." Why such sudden veneration? And why had they not tried this woman in their own court?

Of course, the Master knew why. These men had repeatedly tried to trap Him in His talk, and this was another subtle attempt. If He were to let the woman go, He would be accused of disobeying the law of Moses. And if He were to condemn her to become a bruised and broken corpse buried beneath a heap of stones, He would be branded as "heartless" and a rebel against Rome, which alone could inflict the death penalty.

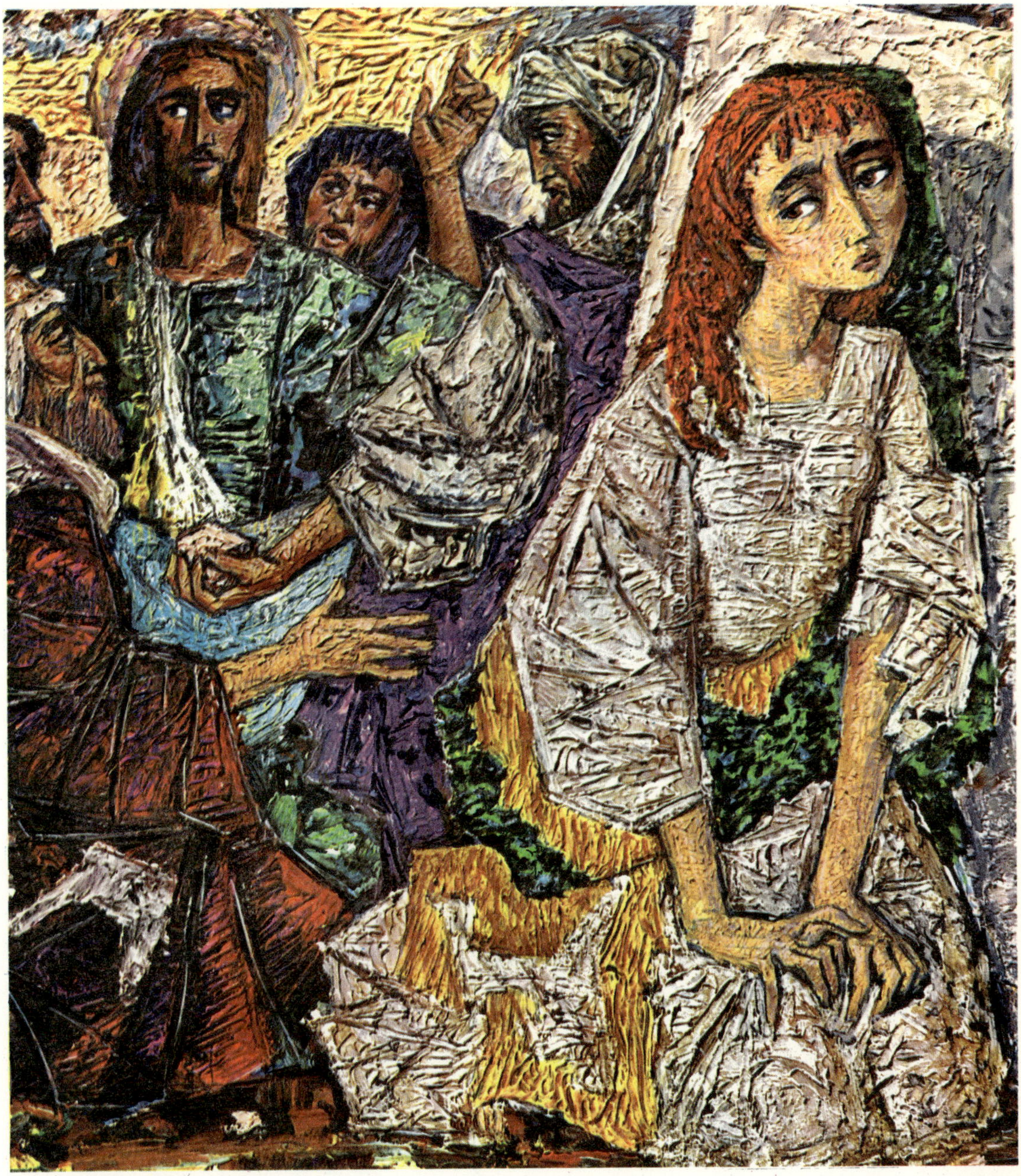

No wonder those haughty eyes gleamed with anticipation. The pharisees felt they had trapped the Nazorean at last!

Remaining seated, the Master bent down and began to trace in the sand with His finger. The eagerness of His opponents mounted. They had Him; they surely had Him! He did not know what to answer them!

"What do you say, Master?" they chorused. After all, He had been teaching as if He had authority! Let Him show His authority now!

Jesus straightened up and looked the most belligerent adversary right in the eyes. "Let the sinless one among you be the first to throw a stone at her."

As the Master bent down to write again, the judges looked at one another in dismay. Jesus had not rejected Moses; He had, instead, perfected him.

Moses had said that the witnesses should cast the first stone; Jesus had said that the judges—and only the innocent among them —should do it.

The older judges shuffled their feet and began to withdraw quietly, one by one. Were they first because they were more guilty or because they were more keenly aware of their defeat? At any rate, their younger companions, suddenly awkward and shifty-eyed, began to drift off in their wake.

They left the woman alone—alone and forgotten, for she had not been their real prey. She stood there before Jesus, making no attempt to run away.

Jesus stopped writing and straightened up. He was no longer indifferent, for He had been sent to seek and to save what was lost.

"Woman," He began, using a term of respect, "where are your accusers? Hasn't anyone condemned you?" For the moment He seemed to ignore her guilt.

And she took heart. "No one, Lord."

"Neither will I condemn you," He continued. And then, that she might not make light of her offense, He added, "You may go, but avoid this sin from now on."

Repentant and filled with hope, she left Him, having drawn from Him new trust in God's mercy and new determination to live by His law. She had received the grace to become a better person. Now it was up to her to correspond.

"He has deposed the mighty from their thrones and raised the lowly to high places" (Lk. 1:52).

MARTHA

LOVING HANDS AND READY FAITH

The Master felt relaxed. Here in the home of Martha of Bethany there were no scribes and pharisees to taunt Him. The atmosphere was one of love and trust. As He stood in the doorway and gazed down the valley, he could hear Martha bustling about behind Him. She was always on the move—a practical, efficient woman who took delight in the management of her home and viewed service as the best proof of love.

Jesus gazed eastward across a jumble of rocky hills, toward the Jordan Valley and Dead Sea. Over there, the Chosen People had first entered the Promised Land. There, too, He had begun His public ministry, and from Mt. Olivet behind Him He would soon ascend to His Father. There was much to

7. Women of the Gospel

think about, for His earthly life was almost over.

Jesus went inside the cool house and sat down to reflect. Mary, who had been flitting about in response to Martha's capable directions, paused beside Him. They began to converse; soon she was sitting on the floor at His feet, all preparations for the meal forgotten.

"Master!" It was Martha's concerned voice. "Doesn't it bother You that my sister has left me to serve by myself? Tell her to help me."

Jesus smiled. He understood His hostess well. She loved Him so much that she would gladly have worn out her hands in His service. She couldn't understand why Mary did not feel the same way. According to Martha, Mary spent entirely too much time dreaming, and should be recalled to her duty. Who could do this better than the Master?

But the Master would not scold Mary.

"Martha, Martha," He chided affectionately, "you are worried about many things, but only one is necessary."

Martha accepted the mild reproof in the spirit in which it was given. Later reflection helped her to see that service is important, but that it loses its meaning without prayer and meditation.

When the Master and His disciples moved on from Bethany, Jesus knew that He would soon return to that pleasant home under extraordinary circumstances.

Several weeks later, when the Master was in Perea, on the far side of the Jordan, a

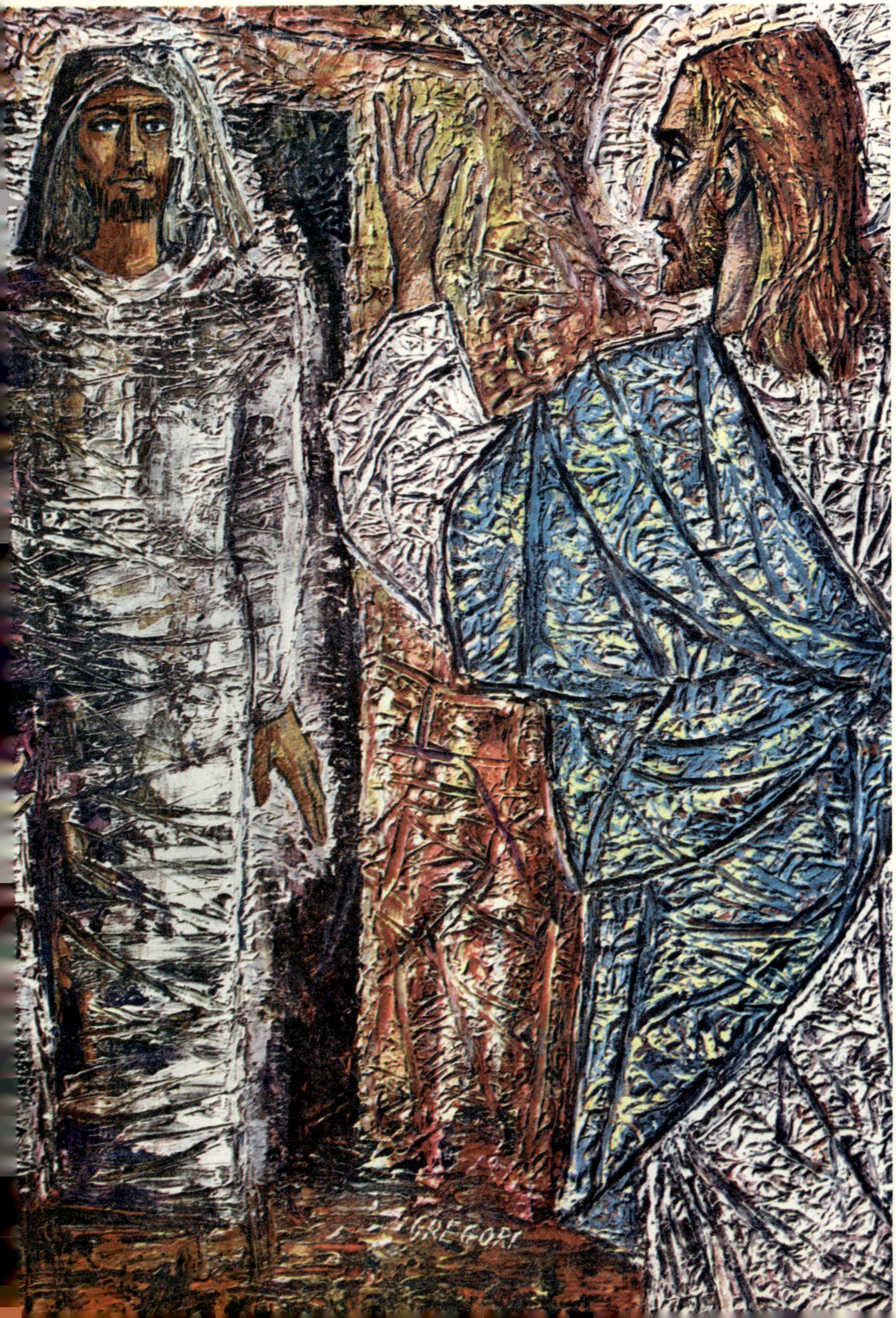
GREGORI

message arrived from the two sisters of Bethany: "The one You love is sick." Right away the disciples knew that the sisters meant their brother, Lazarus, one of Bethany's leading citizens. Martha and Mary must be deeply worried to have sent such a message, yet with great tact they had simply stated the situation without making any request. In their love and trust, they were sure this would be enough.

Yet Jesus merely remarked that this sickness would glorify God and His Son; He gave no sign of intending to follow the envoys as they departed. Nor did He tell the disciples that Lazarus had died shortly after the messengers left Bethany. He lingered on in Perea.

Then, two days later, He announced, "Let us go into Judea!"

The disciples were frightened; they feared for His life and their own. But Jesus reminded them about Lazarus. "He has fallen asleep, but I am going there to wake him," He said.

"Master," they protested, still fearing what the pharisees might do to them, "if he is asleep, he will get better."

Then the Lord plainly told them what had happened, and a shocked silence fell upon the group—a silence broken by Thomas, who declared, "Let us go, too, that we may die with Him!"

When the weary band reached Bethany, the disciples urged Jesus to remain outside the town. Lazarus and his sisters belonged to a well-to-do and influential family, with many upper-class friends and relatives.

Martha's house must be filled with mourners from Jerusalem, any one of whom might put the Master's life in danger by speaking of His return to Judea.

Martha, too, sensed danger. When someone came to whisper that the Master had arrived, she stood up quietly and left the mourners casually, as if going to perform some household task. How relieved she felt as she hurried down the slope to meet Jesus!

"Lord," she exclaimed at once, "if You had been here, my brother would not have died!" It was not a complaint. It was simply a reflection that she and Mary had repeated often during these last four days. The sisters knew that Jesus would do *anything* for them.

As the Master's compassionate eyes gazed into hers, Martha felt impelled to add, "I know, too, that God will give You anything You ask."

"Your brother will rise again," Jesus said seriously.

He must be reminding me of the last, great resurrection, Martha thought. I'll show that I understand.

"I know he will rise again—in the resurrection on the last day."

"I am the resurrection and the life," replied the Master. "Anyone who believes in me—even if he is dead—shall live. And everyone who lives and believes in me shall never die. Do you believe this?"

Martha felt completely at sea. Perhaps Mary would have understood this, she thought, but it's too much for me. Yet, I know it's true. Whatever He says is true. I believe it.

"Yes, Lord," she replied, and she added, "I believe that You are the Christ, the Son of God."

The Master's eyes glowed with joy.

Then Martha thought of Mary, whose sensitive nature cried for consolation even more than her own. "Shall I call her?" she asked.

Jesus nodded, and Martha hurried back up the road to the village.

Impulsive Mary did not leave the other mourners' company unseen. "She is going to weep at the tomb," they murmured, and they followed her.

A shudder ran through the Master's sturdy frame. Mary's sobs and the genuine grief mirrored in the mourners' faces caused tears to well up in His own eyes. "Where have you laid him?" He asked.

Up the slope of Olivet they climbed.

"See how He loved him!" some were exclaiming, as they observed the tears rolling down Jesus' cheeks.

"Couldn't He have kept this man from dying?" others wondered. "After all, He opened the eyes of the blind!"

They reached the tomb, a chamber dug out of the mountain. Sixteen steps led down into it. But the entrance to the stairway had been sealed.

"Take away the stone," Jesus said.

Martha's practicality asserted itself again. "Lord, by this time there must be a stench. It has been four days already."

"But didn't I tell you," He reminded her, "that if you believe, you will see the glory of God?"

What could He mean? Martha did not know, but in her heart she repeated her act of faith: "Yes, Lord, I believe."

While the men were lifting the stone, Jesus raised His eyes and solemnly thanked His Father for what was about to take place. Then, standing at the top of the stairway, He called out to His friend, whose body was decomposing somewhere in the darkness below, "Lazarus, come out!"

There was a stunned silence. Then faint sounds could be heard—shuffling sounds. A gasp rose from the throng. Bandaged from head to foot, a human figure was struggling up those sixteen steps. It stood stiffly at the entrance to the tomb, unable to free itself from its wrappings.

"Unbind him," said Jesus.

Martha gazed at the Master, her eyes shining with joy. Never had she dreamed that faith could be rewarded so fully! And little did she realize that the raising of her brother to life would send her Friend on to His death.

"Has anyone hoped in the Lord and been disappointed?
Compassionate and merciful is the Lord" (Sir. 2:10, 11).

MARY OF BETHANY

EVERYTHING SHE COULD...

They were quite different—those two sisters of Bethany. Martha was practical and steady; Mary, dreamy and impulsive. But they were alike in their reverence for the Master.

It was Mary's devotion that led her to sit at His feet, drinking in His every word. It was Martha's devotion that caused her to bustle about, preparing tasty meals for a weary traveler. Each showed her love in her own unique way.

After the raising of Lazarus, the Master and His disciples withdrew to a peaceful mountain side, overlooking the Jordan Valley. Days passed. The Master's "hour" drew near.

A week or so before the Passover, Jesus and His disciples were again on the move toward Jerusalem. As they made their way down the Jordan Valley, Jesus strode in the lead, head high and eyes ablaze with deter-

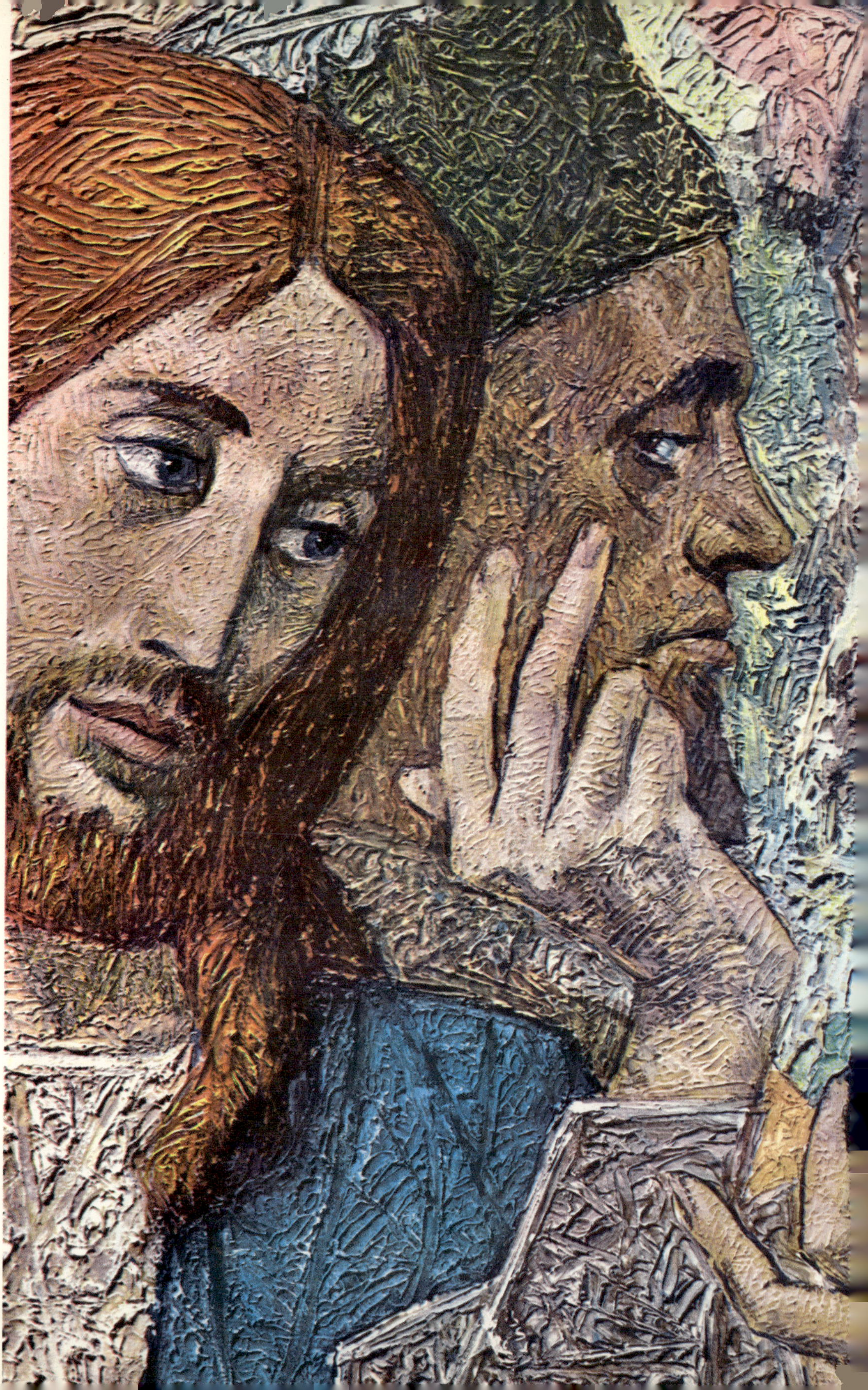

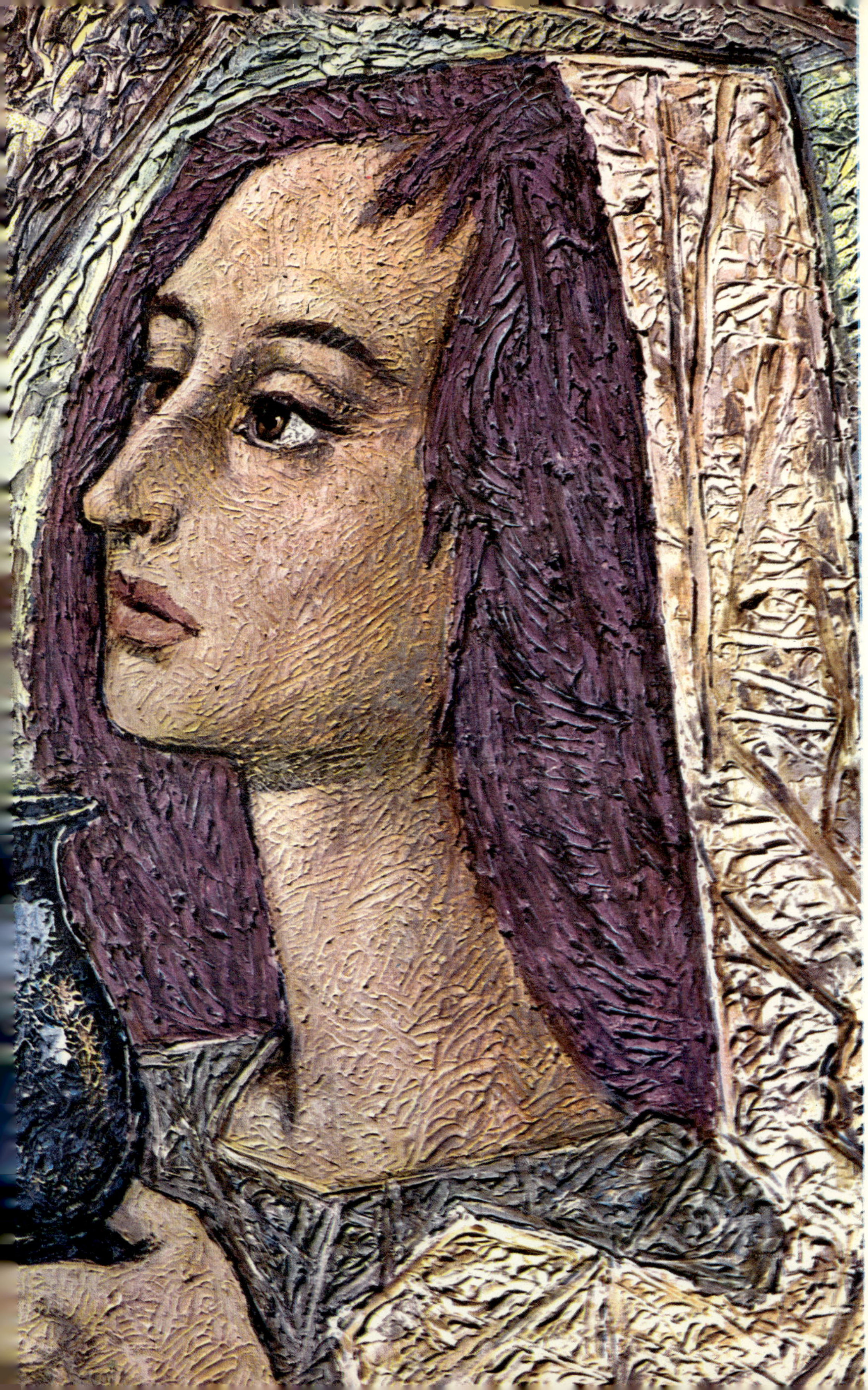

mination. The disciples trailed along behind Him, wonder and fear mixed in their expressions. Were they to walk straight into the clutches of their enemies?

Yes, the Master told His Twelve. The Son of Man was soon to be seized and scourged and crucified. This would take place in Jerusalem. But, Jesus added, He would rise again.

Passing through Jericho, the Master restored the sight of a blind beggar named Bartimaeus and healed the sick soul of a dishonest tax collector named Zacchaeus. He and His disciples then turned westward onto the brigand-infested road of the Good Samaritan parable. Near nightfall, on the Friday before Palm Sunday, they arrived once more in Bethany.

Martha and Mary were overjoyed to see Him again. So, too, were many of the townspeople who had witnessed the raising of Lazarus. As word of His return got about, Simon "the leper" consulted Martha; he wished to hold a great banquet in the Master's honor. Martha joyfully offered her services, and preparations were made.

It was Saturday evening. Jesus, Lazarus, Simon and the apostles reclined at table in Simon's house. Martha and other women served.

As usual, Mary's contribution was impulsive and unique. All of a sudden, she was there in the doorway, where she hovered for an instant before she flew to the Master's side. Her deft fingers broke open the alabaster vessel they clasped. A precious perfume called spikenard poured out upon Jesus' head.

This customary gesture of homage had been performed in an extraordinary way, for Mary's generosity knew no limits. In an instant the fragrance filled the entire room.

Yet there was more that this impulsive young woman could do for the Master. Her vessel had contained a whole pound of the precious perfume, and He was to have it all. She knelt at His feet and poured the remaining contents out upon them. Letting down her hair, she wiped His feet, almost as if wrapping them in a shroud.

The tenderness of the action was not lost to Jesus, who understood Mary's generous love perfectly. But the disciples—especially Judas—grew indignant.

"What a waste!" they exclaimed. "That perfume could have been sold for a great sum and the money given to the poor!"

The Master heard them and could not let the remark pass. "The poor you have always with you," He declared. "You will not always have me." And He added, "By perfuming my body, she is beginning to prepare it for burial. Wherever the Good News is proclaimed throughout the world, what she has done will be told in memory of her."

And so it came to be. Matthew, Mark and John all recount the incident.

The impulsive Mary had shown her love in the best way she knew, and in the sorrowful days of the following week she would be thankful for having taken this opportunity.

"The man without love has known nothing
    of God,
for God is love" (1 Jn. 4:8).

The Widow and Her Mite

THE GREATEST GIFT

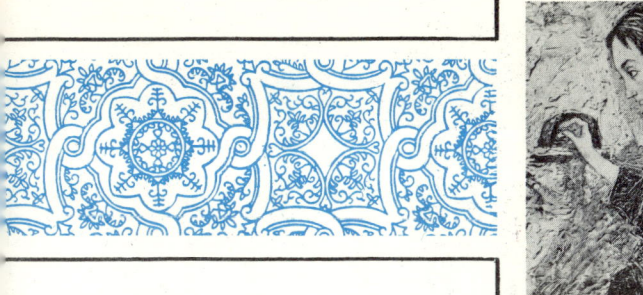

The temple courts were astir with normal, daily bustle. Scribes, pharisees, money-changers and pilgrims swarmed through the great gates, bent on trafficking and praying, bartering and giving alms.

Beneath one of the massive walls stood a series of stone benches. Here the Master sat with His Twelve. The day's encounter with the pharisees had ended. Jesus, however, seemed in no hurry to depart from His Father's house, which He had entered in triumph a day or two before.

The Master's eye fell on a chest of the temple treasury, its trumpet-like mouths gaping to receive the alms of the faithful. As He watched, a rich man came by and poured in his offering with considerable ceremony and rattle. A poor farmer slipped in a few coins that jingled faintly. And then the widow appeared.

THE WIDOW AND HER MITE — THE GREATEST GIFT THE WIDOW

8. Women of the Gospel

She fumbled in the tiny sack that hung at her waist and fished out two half-pennies. The Master watched with compassion. He knew she was about to give her whole living. He understood her, because He, too, was used to giving all He had.

He had begun His giving in the dark, clammy stable of Bethlehem. He had continued it during those years of silent drudgery at Nazareth. Throughout His public mission He had reached out to poor and rich, fellow-citizens and foreigners, righteous and sinful—teaching, healing, encouraging, forgiving. Now He was about to give man His all in the Holy Eucharist and the sacrifice of Calvary.

As the widow dropped her mite into the chest, Jesus called His disciples to witness this living parable. Her gift was especially precious, He told them, because she could not afford to give it; it was all she had to live on.

They understood. That very day they had heard Him censure the proud pharisees for taking advantage of just such poor and generous people. They recognized in her one of the *anawim*, the poor of the Lord, who placed Him before everything else—the people of the beatitudes. Just as giving was the hallmark of the Master, so was it to be the hallmark of His followers throughout the ages.

What can we give to a God who has everything?

Love. Obedience to His law (a law that does not change with the whims of men). Goodness to others, for Jesus declared that whatever is done to the least of His brothers is done to Him.

We can also give God, directly or through humanity:

the cleverness of our minds;

the stored treasuries of our memories;

the hard-won fruits of our education and experience;

the skill of our hands;

the compassion of our hearts;

even patience with our *lack* of talent, health or energy.

Our giving is paradoxical, for, in the words of St. Francis: "It is in giving that we receive." No matter how much we give, God will never let Himself be outdone in generosity.

"Did not God choose those who are poor in the eyes of the world to be rich in faith and heirs of the kingdom he promised to those who love him?" (Jas. 2:5)

CLAUDIA

THE MESSAGE THAT "FAILED"

Claudia murmured, "I know something terrible is going to happen."

"Terrible?" echoed her maidservant. She continued to run the ornate comb through her mistress' long hair. "On a nice morning like this? Surely my lady is mistaken."

"Maybe it *is* my imagination," admitted the procurator's wife. "But never before have I dreamed about such a succession of bad omens."

"By the way," she added, "what was that commotion that made Pilate rise and go down to the praetorium so early?"

"Just a band of rabble. It's a festival day, you know."

Claudia stood up suddenly and walked over to the window. "They're shouting again. What are they saying?"

A seething mass of bobbing heads and waving fists met her gaze. The throng was tightly packed into the space before the praetorium. "He stirs up the people!" someone was shouting. "Away with him!"

117

The procurator's wife turned to her handmaid, who was very busy putting away the combs and cosmetics.

"Do you know more about this than you told me?"

The maid flushed. "I looked out when the crowd came. They brought a prisoner to the procurator. It was Jesus of Nazareth."

Claudia felt the blood drain from her face. "Then my dream did have a meaning. Something terrible is going to happen to Him—and to us!"

"I didn't want to tell you, because I know how you respect this young prophet's teachings.... But my lady's breakfast must be ready. I'll go fetch it."

Claudia nodded absently and began to pace the room. Jesus of Nazareth was a good man—a just man. She knew of the pure and beautiful doctrine He taught and the wonders He had worked to help people. Why, it was said that in the village of Bethany, on the far slope of Mount Olivet, He had raised a dead man to life!

Pilate absolutely must not let anything happen to Jesus! Surely her husband knew better than to call down misfortune on their family. He was well intentioned. But he was also a politician....

"Bring me a writing tablet!" called Claudia as the maidservant reappeared with breakfast. "And send for someone to carry a message to the procurator!"

The wax tablet was brought; the message was swiftly written: "Please don't get involved in the case of this just man, for the dream I had about him last night disturbed

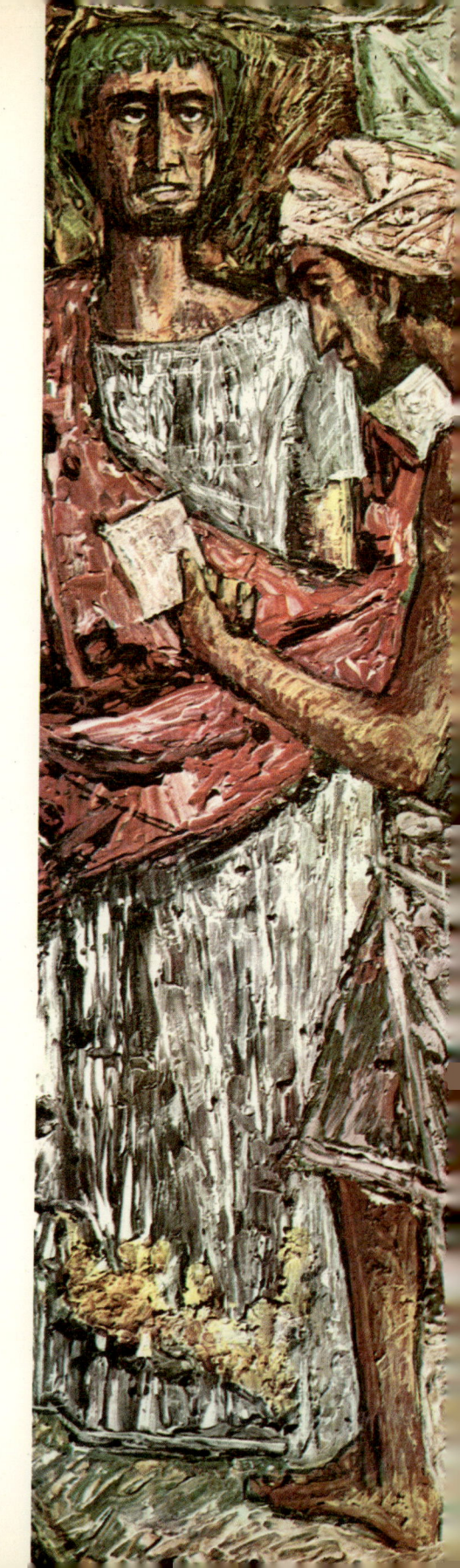

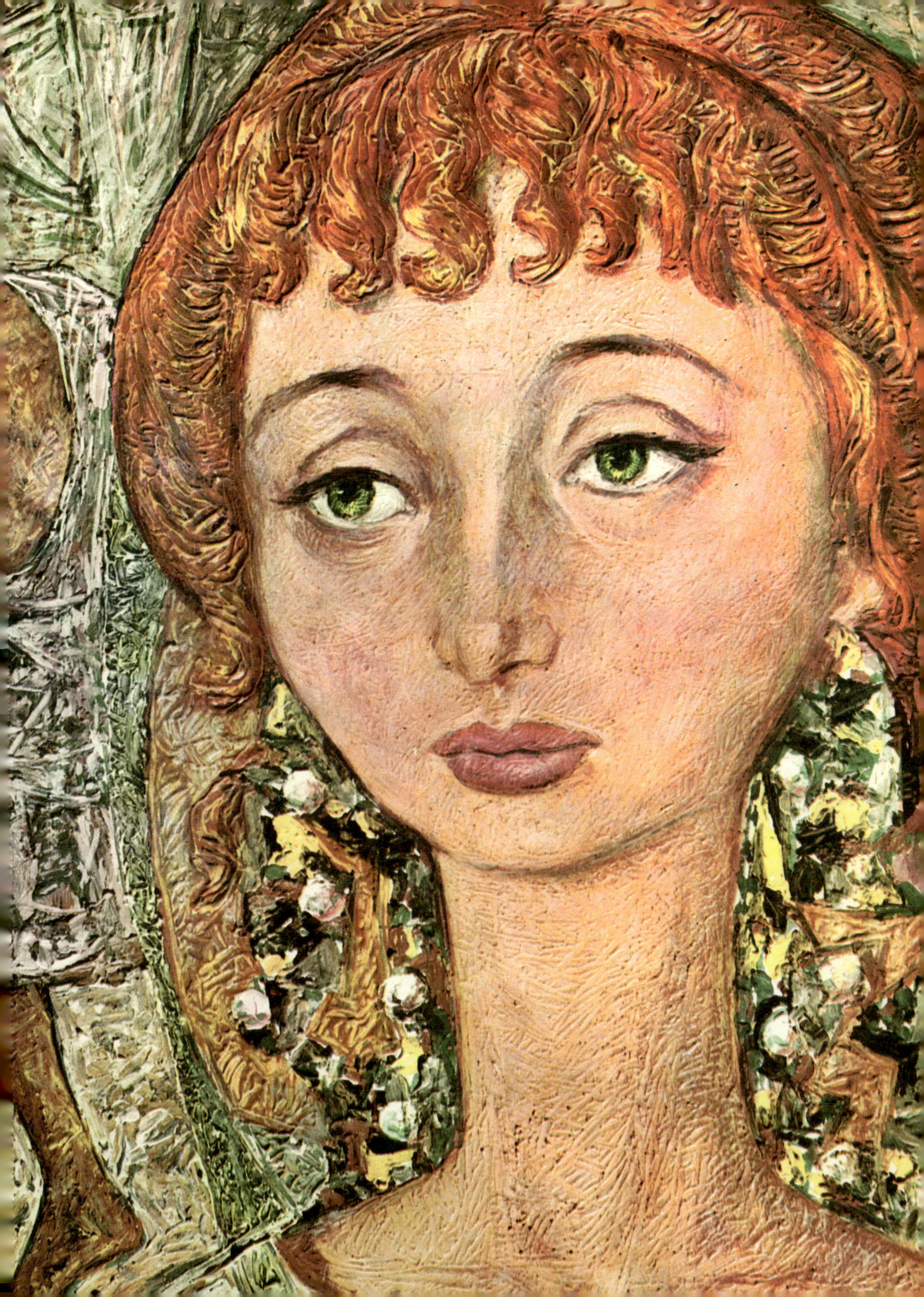

me greatly." Pilate was a man of doubts, of scruples, of superstitions. Surely he would pay attention to such a warning; surely he would not mind her sending it to him while the tribunal was in full session.

A servant left with the message, and Claudia tried to breakfast. But she couldn't eat. She listened tensely, drummed her elegant fingernails on the smooth tabletop and rose to pace the floor again.

A new wave of shouts rose up from the street below.

Claudia feared for Pilate. He meant well, but had so few guiding principles! He was too attached to positions and honors to be really strong of character, like the man from Nazareth....

The morning dragged on. The clamor below waxed and waned, then grew to new intensity. Now Claudia could hear unmistakable shouts of "Crucify him! Crucify him! We have no king but Caesar!" And then, a few minutes later, shrieks of jubilation.

Although her face was buried in her hands, she heard the Master being led away. A few minutes later, she also heard her husband's loud step in the hallway. She dried her tears hastily and pretended to be caring for the fire at the altar of Lares and Penates, the household gods.

Without a word the procurator stomped into the room and flung himself down on a divan. Claudia became even busier with the fire.

"I tried," Pilate mumbled after a few minutes. "I tried more than once."

Claudia left the fire and sank down beside him.

"I even had him scourged so they'd let him go," Pilate continued. His wife drew in her breath sharply, but the procurator pretended not to notice as he added, "But then they told me if I freed him I was no friend of Caesar's. What could I say to that?"

Claudia remained silent.

"They were jealous," Pilate continued. "You could read it all over their faces. The Nazorean was popular. His enemies gathered this mob and riled people up against him."

The noontime air had grown unusually chill.

"I would almost have become one of his followers," Claudia murmured, "but now it's all over...."

"He was a great man," said Pilate. "Too bad...."

"But three days later he will rise" (Mk. 10:34).

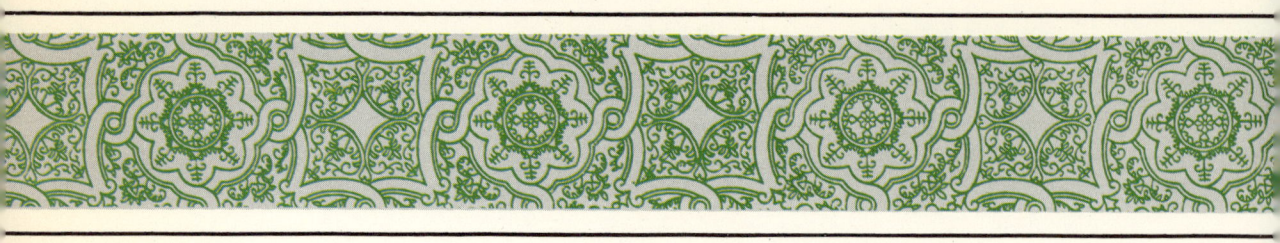

THE WOMEN AT THE CROSS

FAITHFUL TO THE END

It was almost noon. Howls of glee and wails of sorrow arose from the throng that pressed in about three condemned men emerging from the city gate.

No expression or voice was neutral. These people either hated or loved the Man from Nazareth. Word of Jesus' trial and condemnation had whipped through Jerusalem, driving His friends and foes alike out into the streets. Now, outside the walls of the city, they surrounded Him, some clamoring for His death, others mourning its approach.

The Master struggled along beneath His cross, unable to speak to the sympathizers whose voices rose on all sides. His strength was failing; a sweat of blood and an unbelievably barbarous scourging had made Him one, great wound.

"Here, carry this cross!" a Roman soldier ordered roughly. And he thrust forward a passer-by who had been "commandeered" on his way into the city.

THE WOMEN AT THE CROSS — FAITHFUL TO THE END

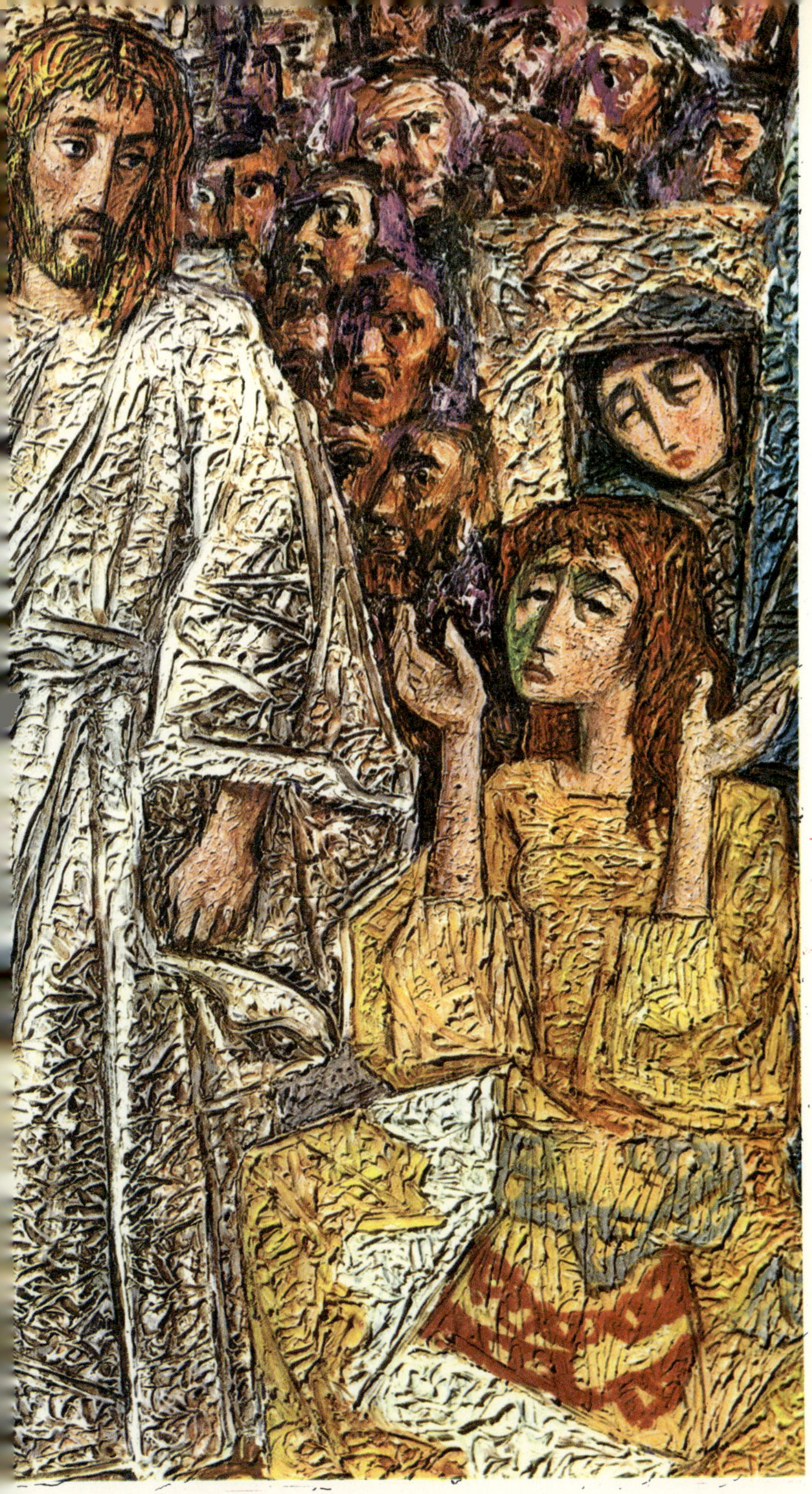

A crossbeam was settled onto the shoulder of Simon of Cyrene. The Master's breathing became less labored. He turned His attention to the group of mourners.

Many were women. Some were young and had small children with them. The Master looked at the children and saw beyond them some thirty-odd years into the future: their generation would perish in the terrible destruction of Jerusalem!

"Don't cry for me," He urged the women gently, "but for yourselves and for your children.... If these things happen to the green wood, what will happen to the dry?"

When the cortege reached Calvary, one or more of the women brought forward the bitter, spiced wine that was always prepared for victims of crucifixion. This drink served as a mild anesthetic. The soldiers gave the mixture to the two thieves; Jesus, however, had chosen to endure His crucifixion in all its agony, so He did not drink. Yet, in order to show His gratitude to those who had prepared the wine, He tasted it.

As the blood-stained garments were torn from Jesus' body, all His wounds seemed to scream in protest. The Master lay down, stretching His arms out upon the great crossbar, and His crucifixion began.

The throng drew back. Neither jeers nor wailing could drown out the heavy thuds of nails being pounded into flesh and the great thump of a cross being settled into place. The sky grew dark.

Some distance from the cross stood a band of the Master's friends and the loyal group of women who had gone about with Him in

Galilee, ministering to His needs. A second, smaller group had obtained permission to approach the cross and was making its way forward. In this group were Mary, the Mother of Jesus, and Mary Magdalene.

His features contorted with pain, the Master gazed down into those compassionate faces and bequeathed His Mother to all mankind in the person of John.

His Mother! How greatly she was suffering with Him in spirit! What veneration she deserved for her wholehearted, lifelong cooperation with the plan of God! Her name would never depart from the hearts and lips of believers down through the ages!

To her, and to all these loyal women who had followed Him from Galilee to Calvary, the Master would grant the reward of seeing Him in His risen glory, of being present at His ascension and of receiving the Holy Spirit at the beginning of a new and wonderful era.

"Whoever acknowledges me before men—the Son of Man will acknowledge him before the angels of God" (Lk. 12:8).

MARY MAGDALENE

AFTER THE SUNRISE

"Did you feel that? The earth just quaked again."

Mary nodded absently. She had only one thought in mind—to reach the tomb and anoint the body. The city walls loomed dark above them as the women passed through the gate in the dim light of early morning.

As Magdalene involuntarily glanced towards Golgotha, a shudder shook her slight frame. Only the day before yesterday it had taken place—the incredible event that had snatched the Master from their midst. The mound lay shrouded in a grayness not unlike the depression that enveloped the entire group of disciples.

Nearby was the spot where she herself had stood with a considerable band of Jesus' friends and followers until she had seen that John was able to approach the cross with the Master's Mother. Then Magdalene, too, had squeezed her way forward to give what comfort she could.

9. Women of the Gospel

If only I could have done more, she thought. I owe Him everything....

The rocks and pebbles underfoot were becoming more visible, and the women could quicken their pace. To be sure, the stone at the tomb's entrance would be difficult to move, but willing hands would not be lacking. Other faithful women followers of the Master were also abroad in the dim light, all bent on coming to render Him this last homage, just as they had first looked after His needs during those wonderful tours of Galilee.

He had done so much for them—healing some of bodily infirmities, delivering others from spiritual slavery, freeing Magdalene herself from seven devils. The little community that had formed itself to minister to Him would not forsake Him now. Leaving their various lodgings in small groups, these loyal disciples were bringing with them spices and perfumes prepared before sundown on Friday, together with oils and ointments purchased last night, after the sabbath had ended. Joseph and Nicodemus and their servants had embalmed the body with an abundance of myrrh and aloes, but upon noting the men's haste, the women had decided that surely the quality of the process could be improved upon!

"Something's wrong!"

Now that they were only a few yards away from the tomb, the women could distinguish a gaping opening. The stone, enormous as it was, had been rolled aside.

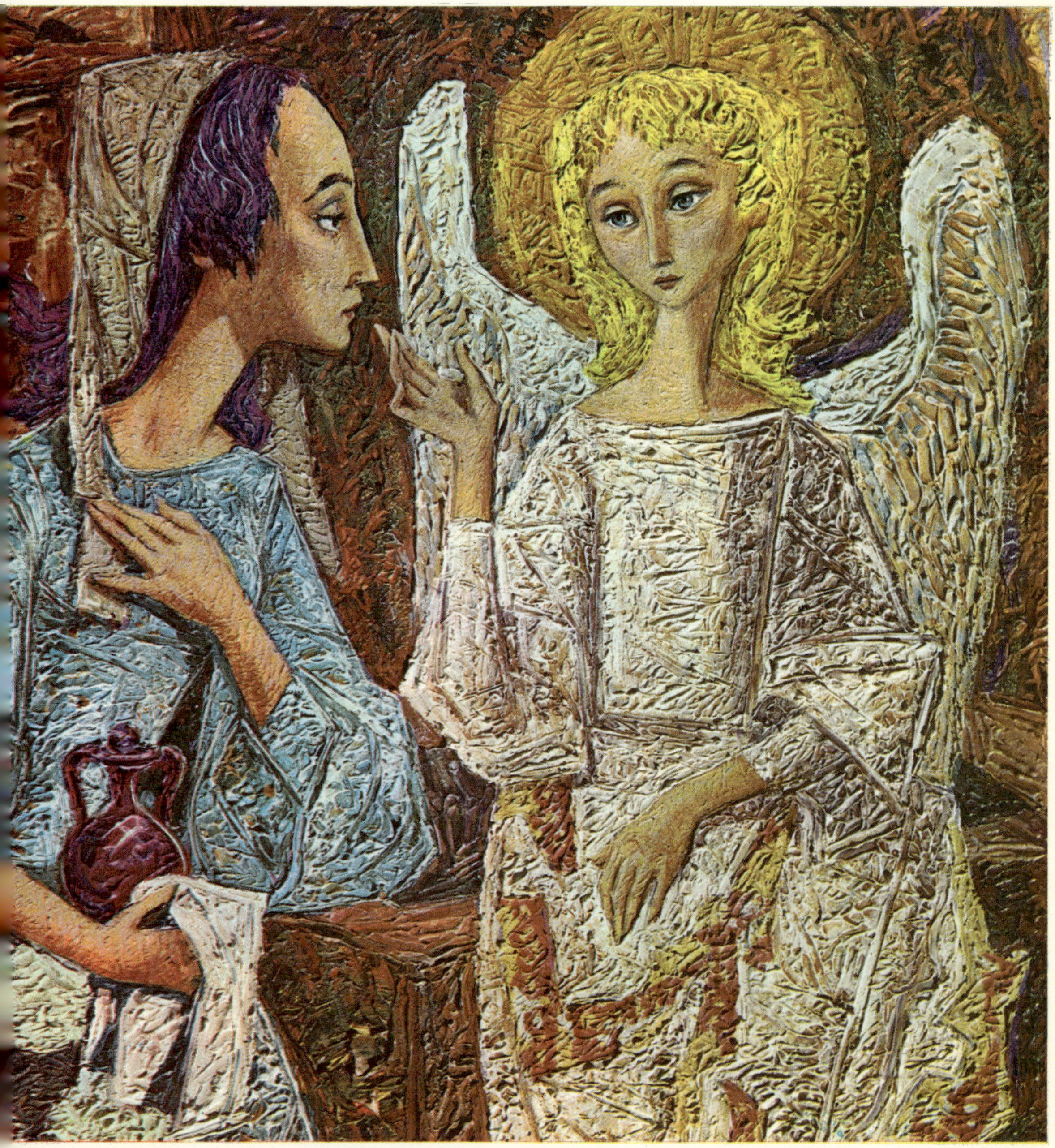

Trembling, they lighted a candle and entered first the vestibule, then the inner chamber. The tomb was empty! There, on the rock ledge where the body had rested, only a folded piece of cloth remained. Other wrappings lay on the floor of the chamber. Otherwise, the sepulcher was empty.

Help must be gotten at once. Without waiting to see whether she would be accompanied, Magdalene rushed out of the tomb and began to run towards the city. The disciples must be told!

Finding Peter and John together, Mary blurted out the story. "We don't know where they've laid Him!" she gasped in conclusion. The apostles hurried out of the house, and Magdalene followed more slowly, still struggling to catch her breath.

By the time she reached the tomb, they had already finished inspecting it and were coming out.

"We're going back to the city," Peter mumbled. He looked dazed. John was completely silent. Mary stifled an impulse to exclaim, "But aren't you going to do something?" After all, what could Peter and John do? Right now they might be hunted men.

She herself would not return to the city. She felt she had to stay as close to the Master as she could, and that meant here in this empty sepulcher. She made her way into the vestibule again and began to weep.

After a while, Magdalene again peered into the burial chamber. Two figures were seated on the ledge, one at either end. They were radiant with light, but neither of them was the Master. Somehow she felt that they belonged to another world. "Woman, why are you crying?" they asked.

"They have taken the Lord away," she answered, "and I don't know where they've laid Him."

Turning almost in desperation, she saw a third figure silhouetted against the morning landscape as he stood at the entrance to the vestibule. Perhaps this was someone who could help! He might be the gardener of Joseph, who owned the tomb.

"Why are you crying, woman? Who is it you seek?"

"Oh, sir," Magdalene stammered, "if you are the one who carried Him off, just tell me where you have laid Him, and I will take Him away!"

She half realized that she wasn't making sense. How far could she carry the body by herself? But the words had tumbled out, and now she held her breath in expectation.

"Mary!" What affection one word contained! And the voice was His!

Somehow, unexplainably, it was Jesus!

"Master!" Instinctively, she cast herself down in adoration and clung to His feet.

He was really there. And she felt more aware than ever of what she had always sensed—the Master was no mere man!

"Don't cling to me," said Jesus. There were things to be done. The Eleven had to be prepared for His visit to them later that afternoon. And they were so slow to believe! "Go to my brothers," He told her—and it was the first time He had ever called the apostles His brothers. "Tell them I ascend to my Father and your Father, to my God and your God."

The sun was bright; the sky was blue; suddenly it was spring all over. Mary hurried back towards the city, intent on her mission of pouring out the story to the disciples. The whole world had to know about it; Jesus was alive; He was risen!

"Go into the whole world and proclaim the good news" (Mk. 16:15).

WOMAN'S SUBLIME MISSION

At this moment when the human race is under-going so deep a transformation, women impregnated with the spirit of the Gospel can do so much to aid mankind in not falling.

You women have always had as your lot the protection of the home, the love of beginnings and an understanding of cradles. You are present in the mystery of a life beginning. You offer consolation in the departure of death. Our technology runs the risk of becoming inhuman. Reconcile men with life and above all, we beseech you, watch carefully over the future of our race. Hold back the hand of man who, in a moment of folly, might attempt to destroy human civilization.

Wives, mothers of families, the first educators of the human race in the intimacy of the family circle, pass on to your sons and your daughters the traditions of your fathers at the same time that you prepare them for an unsearchable future. Always remember that by her children a mother belongs to that future which perhaps she will not see.

And you, women living alone, realize what you can accomplish through your dedicated vocation. Society is appealing to you on all sides. Not even families can live without the help of those who have no families. Especially you, consecrated virgins, in a world where egoism and the search for pleasure would become law, be the guardians of purity, unselfishness and piety. Jesus who has given to conjugal love all its plenitudes, has also exalted the renouncement of human love when this is for the sake of divine love and for the service of all.

Lastly, women in trial, who stand upright at the foot of the cross like Mary, you who so often in history have given to men the strength to battle unto the very end and to give witness to the point of martyrdom, aid them now still once more to retain courage in their great undertakings, while at the same time maintaining patience and an esteem for humble beginnings.

Women, you who know how to make truth sweet, tender and accessible, make it your task to bring the spirit of this council into institutions, schools, homes and daily life. Women of the entire universe, whether Christian or non-believing, you to whom life is entrusted at this grave moment in history, it is for you to save the peace of the world.

—Vatican II

Daughters of St. Paul

IN MASSACHUSETTS
    50 St. Paul's Avenue, Boston, Ma. 02130
    172 Tremont Street, Boston, Ma. 02111
IN NEW YORK
    78 Fort Place, Staten Island, N.Y. 10301
    625 East 187th Street, Bronx, N.Y. 10458
    525 Main Street, Buffalo, N.Y. 14203
IN CONNECTICUT
    202 Fairfield Avenue, Bridgeport, Ct. 06603
IN OHIO
    2105 Ontario St. (at Prospect Ave.), Cleveland, Oh. 44115
    25 E. Eighth Street, Cincinnati, Oh. 45202
IN PENNSYLVANIA
    1127 South Broad Street, Philadelphia, Pa. 19147
IN FLORIDA
    2700 Biscayne Blvd., Miami, Fl. 33137
IN LOUISIANA
    4403 Veterans Memorial Blvd., Metairie,
      New Orleans, La. 70002
    86 Bolton Avenue, Alexandria, La. 71301
IN MISSOURI
    1001 Pine St. (at North 10th), St. Louis, Mo. 63101
IN TEXAS
    114 East Main Plaza, San Antonio, Tx. 78205
IN CALIFORNIA
    1570 Fifth Avenue, San Diego, Ca. 92101
    278 17th Street, Oakland, Ca. 94612
    46 Geary Street, San Francisco, Ca. 94108
IN HAWAII
    1184 Bishop St., Honolulu, Hi. 96813
IN CANADA
    3022 Dufferin Street, Toronto 395, Ontario, Canada
IN ENGLAND
    57, Kensington Church Street, London W. 8, England
IN AUSTRALIA
    58, Abbotsford Rd., Homebush, N.S.W., Sydney 2140,
      Australia